LEAD LIKE A GENERAL

To Aunt Lois,
Thank you for the great geniology
information about our family.
All the Best,
[illegible signature]

LEAD LIKE A GENERAL

PAUL GILBERT

MARQUIS PRESS

SPRINGFIELD, VIRGINIA

Printed in the United States of America

ISBN-13: 978-0615434469

CONTENTS

MEMORIAL

In memory of Fontelle Gilbert, who inspired the best in many.

DEDICATION

I dedicate this book to Laura, Jenna, and Kiera Gilbert who supported and encouraged me in the writing of this book. I would also like to recognize the Board and staff of the Northern Virginia Regional Park Authority. This high-performance group has inspired my thinking about leadership and organizational development.

Introduction

Any large conflict like the Civil War tests so many people in such extreme ways that countless good and bad examples of leadership can be drawn from it. The leadership lessons of any time and place can be distilled and applied to other times, places, and situations. This is how we learn.

In Lead Like a General we will explore stories of leadership from the Civil War and see how they relate to some of the most cutting-edge research about leadership today. Not only will looking at these real-world examples give us insights into what the research is saying; it will also provide a new lens on some of the leaders and events of the American Civil War.

If you are a leader in a business, government, nonprofit, or military organization, at any level, you can benefit from studying great moments—and sometimes failed moments—of leadership to refine your skills and gain insights into how people react and interact. Leadership is a skill that should be studied, practiced, and applied like any other skill. Just as someone with good pitch can only be a great musician through study and practice, a person with leadership potential can only be a great leader if s/he studies, practices, and applies leadership skills.

People are inherently social creatures who like to get together in groups. But to lead a group, you must first be able to provide a vision of what the potential of this group can be, and then understand how people think and interact in order to motivate the group to act collectively in a common direction. The combination of skills and insight needed to achieve this kind of collective action is so complicated that we often assume leadership is God-given. Instead, I believe that leadership skills can be developed and honed by studying any field related to how people think, behave, and organize themselves, for example, organizational management, cognitive functioning, and behavioral science.

Organizations, whether public or private, have the potential to achieve great things when good leadership is exercised, and will exist in a less dynamic way when it is not. This makes management an important profession with a discrete set of skills that are important to develop.

Leadership has always been closely connected to "strategy," a word that comes from the Greek strategia, which means the art of the General. The role of leadership is usually seen as providing the strategy or plan for the group's collective actions. So it is natural to consult military examples to help flesh out issues related to leadership that can be applied to any leader in any organization.

Why the Civil War?

The Civil War took place 150 years ago. It was the greatest conflict our nation has ever experienced. Between three and four million people were drawn into military service and put in extreme circumstances. This combination created many examples of leadership, good and bad.

This book does not attempt to tell the full story of the war. Many great historians have devoted their life's work to this task, and there are wonderful history books devoted to this subject. The stories in this book are individual, personal stories of specific leaders at moments in time where we can clearly see what they did to try to lead their troops.

The Civil War is an important part of our history. In many ways it was the completion of the American Revolution. In 1776, we formed a new nation, but we were not really sure if we were one unit of government or a collection of states in a loose confederation. We had founding documents that made a great deal of how all men were created equal, but we had an economy in a large portion of the country that was dependent on human slavery. The founders had left a significant amount of unsettled business. Between the Revolution and the Civil War, the country was in an increasingly tense state over slavery, with notable flare-ups like the Kansas Border Wars of the 1850s. Unfortunately, it took one of the worst wars in history to resolve these issues and set us on the path we have followed ever since.

Sources

Wherever possible, I have tried to provide first-person quotes from those who lived the war. Rather than the smoothly processed history in many other books about historical periods, my goal is to bring the reader into the moment by using the words of those who were actually there so that you can hear the voices of those who lived through these dramatic times. During the war, many people kept accounts and diaries of the events. In the years following the war, there was a boom in personal biographies and accounts of the conflict. This period of the late nineteenth century and the first decade of the twentieth century was a golden age in publishing, driven by the wealth of material being written about the war between the states.

Regardless of your overall historical knowledge, it is hard not to be drawn in by the personal accounts of how people thought and felt as they worked through these dangerous moments of history. First-hand narratives from the Civil War are very accessible to modern readers. They sounded much like we do, unlike earlier periods of history when the language of the day was not as familiar to the modern ear.

To make the stories more accessible to readers who are not Civil War scholars, I have intentionally tried to refrain from using military lingo or the alphabet soup of unit designation. In most cases, it is enough to know if the players are Northern or Southern to follow the story and see its significance.

Documentation

The historical stories are largely drawn from primary first-hand sources. Many of these sources were found through Google Books. Google has created a vast and searchable library of primary sources and made them more accessible than ever before, even though many of these books have been out of print for more than 100 years. This library is particularly good for sources that no longer have copyright protection.

Historical photos, maps, and other images have come from public domain sources such as the Library of Congress, Wikipedia, and other outlets.

Geography

The Civil War took place in 10,000 locations, from Texas to Tennessee to Pennsylvania to the middle of the Atlantic Ocean. Most of the stories in this book, however, took place within 100 miles of Washington, D.C. Sixty percent of the combat of the Civil War occurred in Virginia, and most of that in the area between Washington and Richmond. This was the front line and center stage of a far-reaching conflict.

Even when the war was "officially" over, conflicts continued. One day after Lee surrendered to Grant at Appomattox, a group of Confederate cavalry attacked the Burke Train Station in Fairfax County, Virginia, 25 miles from Washington. The Union cavalry chased the Confederates across a small river called Bull Run, not far from the site of two earlier and major battles. The next day, Lieutenant Wiltshire said to fellow Confederate Ranger James J. Williamson, "Has it never struck you as being a notable fact that the first fight of the war occurred on Bull Run and the last shots of the war in Virginia were fired on the banks of that same stream?" The story later found its way into Williamson's book, Mosby's Rangers.

Though the first shots of the war were fired at Fort Sumter outside Charleston, South Carolina, the first large battle was the First Battle of Bull Run (Manassas). Or perhaps Wiltshire was referring to the Battle of Blackburn's Ford, fought before First Bull Run and from both banks of the Bull Run River. Northern Virginia was an area of continual fighting throughout the war, and so offers many lessons in leadership from which we can learn.

"General" Demographics

Because the stories in this book are all about senior military officers and Civilian leaders in the Civil War, they are all college-educated white men from the mid-nineteenth century. Although roughly half were Northern and half Southern, it is not what we would consider a diverse group from a twenty-first-century perspective. However, the group had diverse leadership styles and personality types, and as such there is a great deal we can learn from them—lessons that transcend each individual's ethnic, gender, and educational backgrounds.

Each chapter of this book focuses on one of these leaders, most of whom were generals except for John Mosby and President Abraham Lincoln. Mosby rose from private with no military training in the first days of the war to full colonel. He was a remarkable leader in many ways, and it is widely believed that if the war had continued much longer he would have achieved the rank of general. Mosby is also the only leader who is the subject of two chapters of this book. Each of these chapters tells a very different story that illustrates different leadership principles.

Leadership Insights

Each chapter ends with a section on "Leadership Insights." This section uses the historical story to illustrate cutting-edge research that bears on human behavior in leadership-related situations, that is, on how people think, react, and interact. To motivate people to work for a common goal, it takes the best understanding we can have of what moves people. This area of study transcends numerous academic fields, and many of the theories presented in this book are new. But just as doctor need to study the latest medical journal and attorneys need to keep up with recent case laws in their fields, those engaged in leading others should try to stay up-to-date on the latest knowledge in what motivates people.

This book does not propose one theory of leadership, but rather explores numerous theories. Most theories, ideologies, or belief systems illuminate some areas of their focus and obscure others. In my view, a theory is like looking at various layers of an object through a microscope. As you zoom the lens in and out, certain parts of the object come into and out of focus. It would be foolish to take on one theory (focal point) and assume it gives you a complete picture of leadership. Even with numerous focal points, you may not ever get a complete picture, but you have a better chance of getting a more holistic vision. I have tried to bring a diverse assortment of focal points to the question of what motivates people—from the ancient wisdom of Sun Tzu's *Art of War* to the latest research on perception, brain functioning, public polling data, and many other sources—and how one can use these insights to set and achieve winning leadership strategies.

CHAPTER 1

The Power of Momentum: John Mosby

Their hearts pounding with adrenaline, their horses panting from a long day of riding and nearly two miles of being chased by the enemy, the group of nearly fifty Confederate cavalry waited silently behind some fallen trees on the side of the road while 200 Union cavalry raced towards them. It was a cold and wet day in late March with less than two hours of sunlight left.

Many of the Confederates had not known each other long. Some had just met that day. They had come from every possible background: two English soldiers of fortune, one decorated veteran of the Crimean War, one fifty-year-old blacksmith recently turned soldier, some who grew up in the area, and some from other units who signed on with this group for the day to see if they could win a new horse. Not exactly the crack force you'd want while going up against a force four times as large. As if these odds were not bad enough, they were on the edge of the massive Union encampments surrounding the city of Washington—thousands of Union soldiers within a radius of a few miles, and no sizable Confederate force nearby.

Yet this group was supremely confident of its ultimate victory and had actually picked this fight. Essentially waking a sleeping and deadly giant, this small band had earlier attacked the guards of a large Union cavalry base in Chantilly, Virginia, thirty miles from the nation's capital. The Confederates had then retreated, chased by four times the number of Union horsemen spreading out for nearly a mile along the one-lane road, while the Southerners stayed in a tight group just out of range of Union forces.

When they had come over a small hill with the Union force a short distance behind them, their leader, a young captain renowned for his battlefield success, leadership skills, and tactical insights, had formed them into this group that now waited behind the fallen trees to the side of the road. He told his group to draw swords, not because he had any faith in the sword as a weapon but to keep his group from firing a shot until he was ready to spring his trap.

As the first few Union cavalry soldiers crested the hill with their comrades spread out behind them as far as the eye could see behind them, they were attacked from the side by the screaming, charging Confederates. Surely, these were not the soldiers they had just chased? And just as surely, the Union had ridden into an ambush. The leading edge of the Union pursuit turned and galloped in the opposite direction. Those behind them, hearing the pistol shots and seeing the terror in the eyes of their fleeing friends, assumed the worst and also ran in retreat. The whole line of 200 Union cavalry turned from hunter to hunted in a minute.

In less than an hour, five Union soldiers were dead and thirty-six captured, along with fifty horses and supplies. No Confederates were injured. The commander praised the valor of his group. One of his men who helped lead the charge said, "Well, Captain, I knew the work had to be done, and that was the way to do it."

This young captain had no military training. He was schooled in both law and classical studies. But his knowledge of history and his insights into the human condition made him a great leader.

In later life, recalling that moment of waiting in the woods before the overwhelming force that was chasing them came over the ridge, Mosby wrote in his book War Reminiscences, "My success had been so uninterrupted that the men thought victory was chained to my standard. Men who go into a fight under the influence of such feelings are next to invincible, and are victors before it begins."

This wise captain rapidly rose through the ranks to colonel. Aware that Napoleon and Frederick the Great achieved military success by changing the rules of the game, this young officer did the same on that cold dark afternoon on March 23, 1863. The commander was John S. Mosby, the famous Partisan Ranger. Mosby reported this engagement to his commander J.E.B. Stuart, who in turn reported it to Robert E. Lee. On hearing the news of this against-the-odds victory, Lee said "Hurrah for Mosby! I wish I had a hundred like him."

JOHN S. MOSBY

Leadership Insights

First, Mosby was a student of history and drew insights from great warriors of the past, exactly as we will attempt to do in this book. The Civil War—the largest domestic conflict America had ever seen—created many examples of great and terrible leadership. Just as Mosby used his knowledge of the leaders and strategic geniuses of the past to help him hone his skills, we can all learn valuable leadership lessons from his behavior during the Civil War.

In the attack on Chantilly, Mosby was using a number of effective strategies. First and foremost, he had established a track record of success that created great momentum. If he had not fostered a reputation for success and projected the confidence that went with that track record, his group might have assessed their chances in a different light and lost the confidence that was key to their success. People are drawn to a winning team. Members of such a team feel confident, and the actions of such people lead to success, which leads to more momentum. Success (and failures) are waves that, once started, are hard to turn around.

In a 2008 MIT study of executives who projected confidence and optimism nonverbally, Alex Pentland found that success rates were 87% higher in these executives than in executives who did not have positive and energetic mannerisms. Mosby's confidence in himself and his soldiers was clearly a key element in his excellent leadership.

Mosby had led a number of successful missions that took place at night or where he traveled over fields and through forests to get to his target. By attacking a large, well-armed encampment during the day, by a main road, he was changing up his tactics, so his opponents never really knew what to expect. The boldness of the attack ironically led his opponents to believe that it must be a trap.

The momentum generated through Mosby's series of successes, and his varied tactics, would have been appreciated by the ancient Chinese General Sun Tzu, who wrote in The *Art of War*,

> *You fight with momentum. There are*
> *only a few types of surprise and direct*
> *actions. Yet you can always vary the ones*

> *you use. There is no limit to the ways you can win. Surprise and direct action give birth to each other. They are like a circle without end. You cannot exhaust all the possible combinations!*

In any competitive environment, staying unpredictable is an advantage. And in any endeavor, having the momentum of past successes can galvanize and motivate any team.

By leading his pursuers on a long chase, Mosby was betting that their lines would stretch out and thin the force's leading edge, making it easier to repel. He also understood human nature enough to know that by creating fear in the front of a long line of cavalry, he could make the whole line fall.

Central to this success story is also the appropriate use of risk, not in a foolish, uncontrolled way, but in a deliberate one. Appropriate use of risk is the central tool for growth in business. Understanding the market is the best way to assure that the risk is well-placed for the desired impact. Taking on a larger force is inherently risky, but because Mosby both knew the terrain and more importantly knew how his opponent would react and how his group would perform, he was taking a risk that he could handle.

Here's a key point: If one is to understand leadership, it is essential to understand why people are willing to follow some and not others. In Strength-Based Leadership, Tom Rath reveals interesting polling data from Gallup on why people follow. The research found that most followers have four basic needs from their leaders: trust, compassion, stability, and hope. In a war environment of extremes, like we are looking at here, compassion and stability are more difficult to find, but trust and hope are visible.

MOSBY'S RANGERS

Mosby was known to be very honest and, in his post-war career, he blew the whistle on government corruption in several positions he held. Based on this, we can assume that those that he led understood early that he was a person of strong ethical convictions. Rath states,

> *One of our national polls revealed that the chances of employees being engaged at work when they do not trust the company's leaders are just 1 in 12. In stark contrast, the chances of employees being engaged at work are better than 1 in 2 if they trust the organization's leadership.*

Hope is generated from leaders taking the initiative rather than just reacting to the situation.

Using the same Gallup leadership study, Rath reported that when leaders made the employees feel "enthusiastic about the future" they were 69% likely to be engaged in their jobs. Compare this to 1% engagement when leaders did not inspire hope. Mosby was a master at taking the initiative and fighting only when and where he chose to, and doing so with great success.

In these chapters, you will be able to see a theme: the best leaders are able to give their followers trust and hope, and thereby win the support of those that they are directing.

Mosby was a master of the asymmetrical fight, and more importantly, of understanding how to give a group of people what they needed to rise to new levels and follow him to success. Although he did not fight in large strategic battles, he was able to tie up tremendous Union forces that would have been able to be deployed in winning the war if it were not for his elusive hit-and-run tactics. Sun Tzu's ancient work the *Art of War* foretold what would come to be Mosby's strategy:

> *Make the enemy's troops surrender.*
> *You can do this fighting only minor battles.*
> *You can draw their men out of their cities.*
> *You can do it with small attacks. You can*
> *destroy the men of a nation. You must keep*
> *your campaign short.*

You can look at Mosby's victories as being psychological in nature. He understood his strengths and the blind spots of his competitors better than they did, and took advantage of those opportunities.

CHAPTER 2

Understanding Your Own Reactions: George Custer

As we saw in Mosby's attack on Chantilly, the willingness to take risks was essential to success. Without that willingness, he would have never created a reputation for winning against the odds and would not have inspired the essential confidence in his group. Mosby carefully considered his strategic position and that of his opponents, frequently changing his mode of operation to stay unpredictable.

Unlike Mosby, sometimes we react to external stimuli in predicable, and not productive, ways.Risk can be taken in a foolish rather than in a strategic way. These reactive patterns can cause difficulties.

Take George A. Custer, for example. We all know the story of Custer's last stand: he leads his troops to total massacre by Native Americans at the battle of Little Big Horn in 1876. During the Civil War, Custer also engaged in foolish risk taking, which also caused those he commanded to lose their lives.

On June 17, 1863, 23-year-old Captain Custer arrived at the Battle of Aldie, less than 10 miles down the same road where Mosby had fought his battle months earlier. The quaint village of Aldie, Virginia, known for its

ALDIE MILL

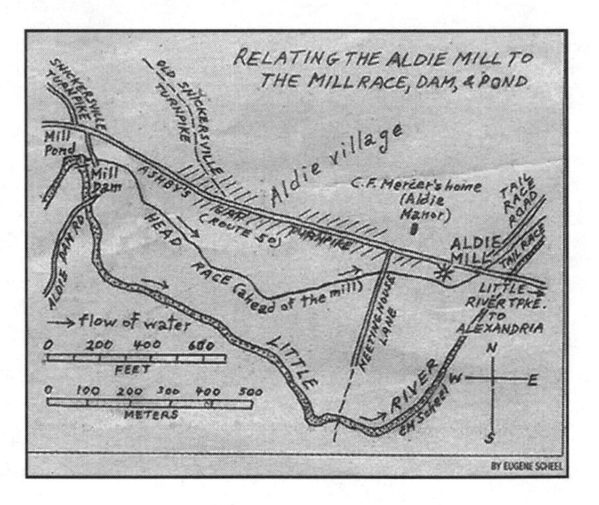

VILLAGE OF ALDIE

large stone grist mill, is about four blocks long. In the Civil War it was situated on what was then the Little River Turnpike (and what is today Route 50). The strategic importance of this little hamlet is that it sits at a gap in the low Bull Run Mountains. Some distance to the west Lee's Army was moving north towards Gettysburg, and to the east Union cavalry were looking for the Confederate army to gain intelligence about where they were going.

On that June day, with temperatures in the 90s, the idyllic village of Aldie had turned from idyll to hell. Custer, who graduated last in his West Point class, arrived at the western edge of town, where Snickersville

Turnpike branches off to the north, to find a battle raging between nearly 2,000 Union and 2,000 Confederate cavalry. Soldiers had been fighting for more than three hours up and down the main street and into the neighboring farmland on Snickersville Turnpike. Waves of horsemen armed with pistols and swords pulsed back and forth in pitched combat while, up the hill on Snickersville Turnpike, behind a stone farm wall, Southern sharpshooters picked off the soldiers in blue.

An account by Captain Charles Francis Adam, Jr., the grandson and great grandson of U.S. presidents reported this:

> *My poor men were just slaughtered and all we could do was to stand still and be shot down. I was ordered to dismount my men to fight on foot...and in a second the rebs were riding, yelling, and slashing among us.*

One can only imagine the smoke, noise, and chaos of nearly 4,000 combined cavalry fighting in such a confined area. Though the cavalry forces waging battle along the main street and in the nearby fields were evenly matched, the sharpshooters behind the stone wall were a force the Union was unprepared to defeat.

Shortly after arriving on the scene, the young aggressive captain rallied the Union forces and charged against the entrenched sharpshooters behind the stone wall. He was successful in breaking the Confederate line and shifting the momentum to the Union. But in his great enthusiasm, Custer outran his troops and found himself surrounded by enemy soldiers. His wide-brimmed straw hat—a hat that closely resembled what many Southerners were wearing—tricked the Confederates into

BATTLE OF ALDIE

thinking he was one of them while he fought his way back to the Union line. Imagine the thick fog of charcoal gray smoke that surrounded him and the others in Aldie, fog created from the actions of 4,000 soldiers firing their black powder rifles and pistols in a confined space for hours of intense battle, making it hard to distinguish blue from gray.

Though Custer was experienced in battle, having fought in the First Battle of Bull Run (Manassas) and seen action in the Peninsula Campaign, the Battle of Aldie could be considered Custer's First Stand. Custer's charge in this battle had mixed results, and it can be argued that Custer's charge against the well-defended sharpshooters had more to do with testosterone than with tactics. On the one hand, Confederate forces moved back towards Middleburg to carry on the fight the next day, making this a modest Union victory. On the other hand, the North's body count was astonishingly high. Union commander Colonel Munford reported, "I do not hesitate to say that I have never seen as many Yankees killed in the same space of ground in any fight." The Union lost 305 men that day; the Confederates had lost only 119. According to O.M. White, who rode with Custer that day, the 1st Maine Cavalry lost 198 out of 294 men.

After the battle, the wounded were sent to makeshift hospitals all over Northern Virginia. Some were sent by train, and a wagon to what was known as the Mansion House Hotel in Alexandria. This was one of the largest hospitals in the region, and behind the wooden facade was the stone Carlyle House Mansion, that had been build in 1752 and played a central role during American Revolution and French and Indian War.

At this stage in the war, the Union was looking for heroes, and a reporter from the New York Times who was at the battle deemed Custer a hero. "As for the Battle of Aldie, there was the bravest qualities of our soldiers exhibited there," the reporter wrote. "One young standout was Captain George Armstrong Custer, a staff officer of Gen. Pleasonton's, who was in the center of the battle and personally led several charges upon the enemy." Within three weeks, Custer was promoted from Captain to Brigadier General, becoming at age 23 the youngest general in U.S history.

James Longstreet

Custer's record throughout the war is filled with acts of personal heroism, but not always good judgment. On the last day of the war, as Grant and Lee were discussing terms of surrender at Appomattox, Custer nearly became one of the war's last casualties when he rode up to the Confederate lines alone—and with no approval from Sheridan or any other commanding officer—to demand the surrender of the whole Army of Northern Virginia.

"Suddenly a horse came clattering along my front. I looked up and saw a smart-looking officer with yellow hair streaming behind him, hurrying forward to where I stood," Southern General James Longstreet recounted in an 1879 interview. "Then [the officer] wrenched him suddenly to his haunches and said, in a somewhat violent tone: 'In the name of General Phil Sheridan, I demand the instant surrender of this army!'"

"I am not the commander of this army," Longstreet had replied, and if I were I should not surrender to you," as Custer was not the commander of the Union forces.

Longstreet then informed Custer that Lee and Grant were meeting, of which Custer seemed to be unaware.

"[Custer] grew pleasant then," Longstreet continued, "and after a while galloped off. He was a brave and spirited young fellow, but my old veterans were not in a mood to humor him when he dashed up to us that day."

GEORGE CUSTER

Leadership Insights

Everyone has triggers that cause predictable reactions. Some people get defensive when questioned. Some become peacemakers when others disagree. Others anger easily, or seek to disengage. The combinations of triggers and reactions are extensive and many of them are rooted in our early family dynamics and experiences.

Custer's reaction to conflict was to attack, but he attacked with recklessness. This served his career for a time, when his army was desperate for a hero, but ultimately the odds caught up with him—soldiers who served under him faced particularly hazardous duty conditions.

Clearly, Custer was not operating at his best. His knee-jerk reaction to conflict did not appear to be made rationally, with full consideration of the circumstances at hand. Predictably, this behavior pattern created undesirable outcomes.

To be your best you must become aware of your own habitual reactions, and first consider the dynamics of a situation before reacting, so that you can take calculated action. Not to do so can create unhealthy decision-making patterns, as recent brain research shows.

Professor Dan Areily of Duke University, for instance, has written about people making irrational decisions in a time of great emotional stress. When this happens, the brain creates a pattern that is likely to be followed in future situations, making the same or similar decisions repeatedly, even if the circumstances are different.

The study to which Areily refers used a simple test. Study confederates told subjects that they had $20 and were willing to give them $5, with the confederate keeping $15. If the subjects said "no," both get nothing. The rational choice is to take the offer and get something. Those who were exposed to positive images before the test usually took the offer. Those who were exposed to negative violent images before the test were more likely to take the less rational and spiteful decision, denying the tester gain, even if it meant they also lost. The interesting element of this study was that once the irrational decision was made, those people were more likely to make the same kind of irrational decision in similar tests, even when no violent images were presented. A negative cognitive pattern had been established.

Leaders need to be aware of their own cognitive patterns and how these patterns might lead to irrational decision making. Custer, for instance, seemed to have developed a pattern of charging head-on toward whatever enemy he faced. In the Civil War, with hundreds or thousands of reinforcements behind him, this behavior worked for him, although it was deadly for his followers. But when he was in the West without abundant reinforcements, his behavior pattern became truly disastrous.

While our reactive patterns may not be as extreme or deadly as Custer's, everyone has triggers that set off well-habituated reactions. If we are not aware of our own reactions, we will assume that these actions are well-thought out and make decisions that might not be good for us or our teams. We will also be destined to replay the same kind of drama in our lives again and again.

Avoiding this trap is not easy. First, we need self-knowledge. Because we tend to believe our actions are justified, and correct, gaining a true understanding of our own cognitive patterns might take some digging. Think about how you have acted under stress, and if those actions have followed a predictable pattern. Bringing that pattern to consciousness is the first step to rising above these reactions.

Interesting fact: our minds do not understand negative messages. So it would have done Custer no good to tell himself, "I will not charge…I will not charge." However, he could have worked to intentionally replace the "charge" reaction with a positive alternative. He could have re-programmed himself by saying something like, "When I am in danger, I will consider at least three options before taking action." This approach would not have eliminated the option of charging but rather made it one of several options to consider before committing himself and his group to action.

Facing undesirable behavior and deliberately working to reprogram your response with a positive or neutral reaction to the stimulus is known as cognitive-behavior therapy. It is widely used to help people with a wide range of issues including mood, anxiety, personality, eating, substance abuse, and psychotic disorders. Anyone can use the same basic process to reprogram any reactive response that is getting in the way of achieving the best.

In the end we control only our own actions, and to be our best those actions need to be thoughtful. You can only become a thoughtful leader through becoming aware of your own reactive patterns and then overriding the old "program" with one that allows you to make the best decisions for the unique situations and circumstances in which you find yourself.

CHAPTER 3

The Perfectionist's Dilemma: George McClellan

On November 1, 1861, George B. McClellan was to save the Union. The thirty-four-year-old General had just been promoted to the dual role of general in chief (top military leader of the whole army) and commander of the Army of the Potomac, the main Union Army in Maryland/Washington/Virginia. On receiving this enormous assignment, McClellan told President Lincoln, "I can do it all."

Most people in the fall of 1861 agreed with him. McClellan had graduated early from West Point, second in his class. He had served with distinction in the Corps of Engineers during the Mexican War and had been a U.S. military observer with the British in the Crimean War. Then he'd left the military and served as the president of a railroad company, so he was used to being CEO of a large organization.

When McClellan took command, the Army of the Potomac was both disorganized and demoralized after being defeated at the First Battle of Manassas. When McClellan arrived in Washington, he found "no army to command, only a mere collection of regiments cowering on the banks of the Potomac, some perfectly raw, others dispirited by the recent defeat."

McClellan wasted no time in bringing his education and experience to the job of building a first-rate army. He saw that the soldiers were well-equipped and trained; he oversaw the building of fortifications and worked to assure good supply lines. In many ways, he was the perfect person for the job. He had a commanding presence and a great intellect, and he was a good manager. The troops loved him for making them into a real army, an army that was well-provisioned and could do all the maneuvers that any professional army was supposed to know at the time.

Yet the perfectionism that let him build a finely tuned army from raw recruits also made it impossible for him to complete his assignment and win the war.

His entire career to this point had seemed like a chain of successes, but he was terrified of failing. As a result, he consistently overestimated his enemy's strength, often doubling their real numbers. Although he had the power to win, he took defensive rather than offensive positions, because he could not be assured that every element was perfect.

He obsessessed over details, blocking his ability to think strategically and act decisively. When he was first assigned command of the Army of the Potomac, he ordered his generals to focus on details that should have been delegated much further down the chain of command. In orders to his general officers on August 4, 1861, for instance, he commanded that the men "carry in their knapsacks only a change of underclothing, an extra pair of shoes, towel, soap, etc. The blanket and shelter tent will form the rest of their load." In the same set of orders, he instructed his officers, in exacting language, that cavalry may only be used in open country and never in the woods or along a "road skirted by timber," as if such precision were possible in a wide-ranging war, and particularly in the rural landscape of the 1860s. He gave his officers enormous volumes of highly detailed orders on every conceivable detail and potentiality.

None of these details was meant to be best management standards, but precise orders about everything from guard shifts to toiletries that were to be followed to the letter of the law.

With his eye for detail and great administrative skills, McClellan could have been a great asset to any large organization that was looking for improved operational efficiencies and some modest internal growth. But his own perfectionism made him incapable of aggressive action. All the details were never quite in an order perfect enough to move to the next step.

McLellan and Staff at Upton Hill

Afraid to move far into the Virginian country outside Washington because of having overestimated Confederate strength, McClellan's star began to fade when the Southerners withdrew from their fort at Upton Hill a few miles from Washington and the North discovered that the large cannons they had seen from a safe distance were Quaker guns—logs painted to look like cannons. Shortly after the Upton Hill Quaker gun incident, Congressman Lyman Trumbull from Indiana said of McClellan, "Young Napoleon is going down as fast as he went up."

Quaker Guns

Under pressure to dislodge the Confederate army stationed in and around Manassas, McClellan took months to come up with a plan. Instead of simply engaging the much smaller force just

30 miles from Washington, he proposed to transport his entire army by river boats eighty miles to the south.

He planned to draw the Confederate army in Manassas south to defend Richmond. McClellan figured he could either take Richmond before they arrived, or fight the rebel army on an open field of his choice. It was an overly complicated solution to a simple problem, and one with little or no strategic advantage. As Lincoln pointed out, he would be "only shifting, not surmounting a difficulty," since he would be facing the same enemy army either way. While the General was arguing the merits of this elaborate plan, the Confederate Army in Manassas withdrew to a better defensive position forty miles farther south behind the Rappahannock River. Later insections of the abandoned fortification in the Manassas and Centreville area revealed more wooden Quaker guns like the ones at Upton Hill, and it was clear that once again McClellan had vastly overestimated his enemy and lost opportunity through inaction.

Still in love with his original plan to load a 100,000-man army onto boats and send them down to the Yorktown/Williamsburg area, McClellan pushed to continue his strategy, even though the goal of dislodging the forces at Manassas had changed. Lincoln, wanting to see some kind of action from the brilliant administrator who would not act, allowed him to go forward with the plan. The result was the Peninsula Campaign.

This campaign followed the same pattern. Despite a larger and better equipped army, McClellan continually overestimated his foe and delayed engagement until all conditions were perfect which, of course, never happens. As a result the Peninsula Campaign became a costly failure for the Union.

Leadership Insights

Research on brain function has helped us understand individual differences in how we process and act on information. The four quadrants of the brain all function quite differently and help to explain these differences. In George McClellan's case, it is quite obvious where his strengths and weaknesses were. He was obviously very intelligent, but with a strong dominance in the lower (limbic) left quadrant of the brain.

GEORGE MCCLELLAN

This quadrant is focused on organizational, administrative issues and is inherently controlling, detail focused, conservative, and highly risk averse. This is extremely linear thinking.

One could not find a better example of lower-left thinking than George McClellan, and it is clear that his strengths and weaknesses are flip sides of the same coin. He was brilliant in planning, uninspired in strategy, and nearly completely unable to take the risk inherent in action.

By contrast, Robert E. Lee, the polar opposite of McClellan, would have likely scored very high on upper (cerebral) right brain function. The upper right is known for holistic, strategic, and imaginative thinking.

Someone with dominance in this area can envision many steps ahead and see many possible solutions to any problem, but may not be as focused on the details. (Later in this book we will look at the strengths of the Lee/Jackson/Stuart team, how well they functioned together, and how Lee's strategic visions were not able to be well-implemented when he lost the team that pulled in different strengths.)

Cerebral Left	Cerebral Right
Analytical Logical Problem Solving	Strategic Intuitive Synthesizing
Limbic Left	**Limbic Right**
Administrative Planning Controlling	Emotional Social/Helping Expressive

Herrmann's Whole Brain Model. Source: Herrmann, N. (1996). Herrmann whole brain model. The Whole Brain Business Book. New York: McGraw-Hill.

The Herrmann Whole Brain Model is a popular tool for understanding the brain's four quadrants. This model (Figure 4) looks at each quadrant's dominant functions. Every individual has a different combination of dominances.

If Lincoln had understood individual differences the way brain dominance research explains them today, he could have used McClellan's great talents at administration and organization (limbic left quadrant) to build, supply, and train a first-rate army, and select someone else with more strategic aptitude (cerebral right) to lead this well-oiled machine in battle. As leaders, it is important to understand your own brain strengths (and perhaps hidden weaknesses). You'll also be a better leader if you apply this understanding to those around you, so that you can use peoples' strengths more effectively.

CHAPTER 4

Strategic Timing and Great Teams: Ulysses S. Grant and Robert E. Lee

One cannot think about leadership and the Civil War without thinking about Ulysses S. Grant and Robert E. Lee, the two great generals who had overall command of the Union and Confederate armies respectively for at least the last half of the war. While the differences between these two were great, it is interesting to look at some of the ways their leadership styles were similar.

To examine this, we will look at arguably the greatest victory of each. For Grant it was Vicksburg in northwest Mississippi, and for Lee it was Chancellorsville, west of Fredericksburg, Virginia.

Both campaigns happened in the spring and summer of 1863, and their successes put the generals on a path that would bring them together in direct conflict at the conclusion of the war.

Each campaign was different, yet each featured notable similarities in strategy and leadership.

Vicksburg in brief

Located on the Mississippi River, Vicksburg was a Confederate industrial and economic center in what was then called the West (west of the Appalachian Mountain range). Vicksburg was close to Jackson, Mississippi, the state capital, and the area was a Confederate stronghold.

ULYSSES S. GRANT

To win this campaign, which Grant saw as essential for victory in the war, he would need to do several key things: (1) take his fleet of iron-clad gunboats past heavy fortifications; (2) move a large army across the great Mississippi river; and (3) fight off two Confederate armies in the area, one commanded by General Pemberton in Vicksburg, and one commanded by General Johnston in the City of Jackson. These two armies nearly matched the number of Grant's forces, and they had the home field advantage of strong defensive positions and supplies.

To get the river boats past fortifications, Grant let the current float them down the river at night. Although Confederate cannons blasted the Mississippi, most of the fleet floated past the defenses unharmed. Then, when it came time for his army to cross the river, Grant distracted his foe with both an amazing cavalry campaign led by Benjamin Grierson deep into Mississippi to cut off Confederate supply lines, and a diversionary attack by Sherman and a small force. The two distractions had their effect; Grant crossed the river with only token opposition. Then, instead

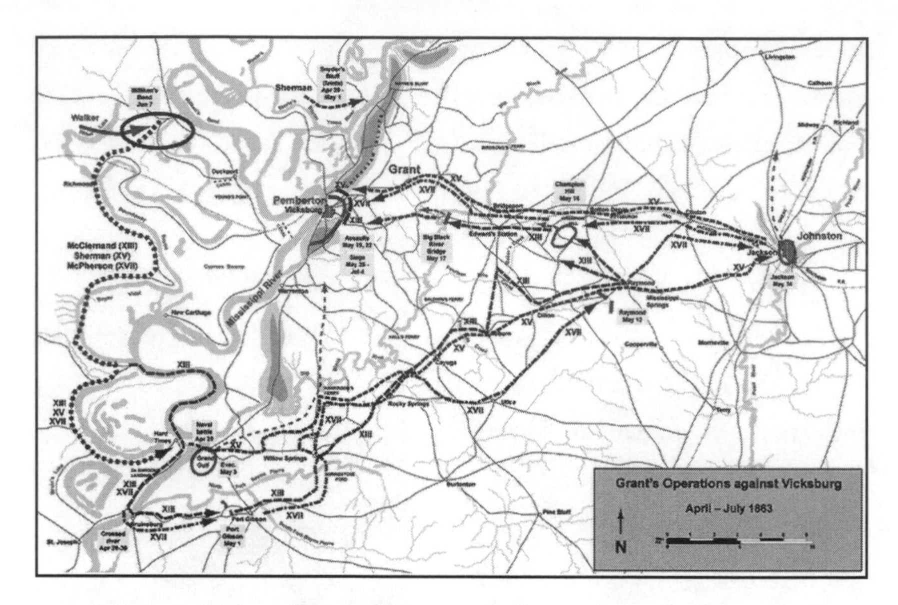

BATTLE OF VICKSBURG

of moving straight for Vicksburg, Grant hit the city of Jackson and was able to knock out the forces that General Johnson was recruiting and training there.

In a little over two weeks, the Union army marched 180 miles and successfully fought five battles, defeating two Southern armies and denying the South one of its few centers of industry.

Chancellorsville in brief

Along the Rappahannock River in and around Fredericksburg, Virginia, Lee waited behind defensive trenches with 60,000 troops. Meanwhile, General Joseph Hooker, advancing from the north, was determined to crush Lee's army with his force of around 110,000 men.

Hard-drinking and feisty, Hooker told his troops "May God have mercy on General Lee, for I will have none." Hooker was expecting Lee to retreat or fight defensively. He did not expect Lee to leave a small force to defend Fredericksburg and use most of them to launch an offensive

Robert E. Lee

against Hooker's superior army. The two forces clashed west of Fredericksburg, and Hooker ordered his troops to retreat to defensive positions around Chancellorsville, a few miles away. That night, as Lee and Stonewall Jackson sat around the campfire discussing how to continue their push, J.E.B. Stuart, the head of Lee's cavalry and his chief source of intelligence, reported that while most of the Union army occupied good defensive positions, the right flank was "in the air."

With this news, Lee stayed with only 15,000 troops to face Hooker's main force. He sent General Jackson with 30,000 troops on a 12-mile march over backroads and through

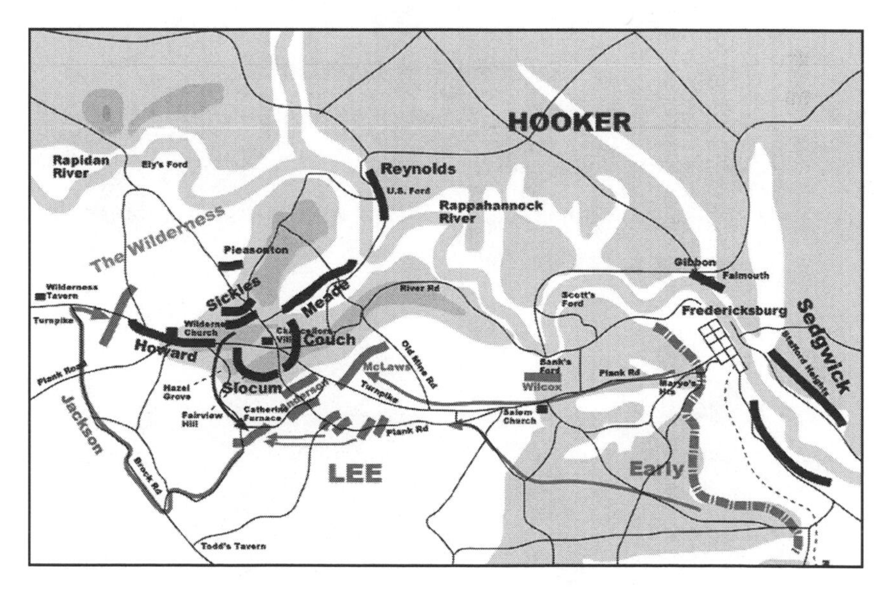

Battle of Chancellorsville

dense forest to attack Hooker's disorganized right flank. Jackson's move was largely undetected, and Hooker took the few reports he'd heard of Southern troop movements as signs that Lee was retreating.

As Union forces were preparing their dinner, Jackson's forces attacked from the forests that the Northerners thought were too dense to worry about. By nightfall, Jackson's forces had rolled up the side of the Union lines for two miles. Fighting continued into the night. Trying to keep the momentum of the rout, Jackson and some of his officers rode beyond the Southern lines to plan where they should go next. As they rode back to their troops in the darkness, they were mistaken for Union cavalry and Jackson was shot by his own soldiers, dying eight days later of his injuries.

The next day, the South continued to press the advance and Hooker retreated further, although Union General Sedgwick almost took Fredericksburg. On hearing the news that Hooker's army had been beaten and had retreated to the north, President Lincoln responded, "My God, my God, what will the country say?"

Leadership Insights

Some of the commonalities in Lee's and Grant's leadership include

- The power of strong leadership teams.
- The ability to see opportunities and act quickly to gain momentum.
- The use of strategic timing.

Strong Teams

On one level, this chapter is about two generals. On another level, it's about two leadership teams. Each team member had different areas of strength. Creating a team out of people who have complementary skills and aptitudes effects great achievement.

People are often thrown together into groups. They then have to create a good team with what they have to work with. Under these circumstances, the lead person needs to assess others' skills, deploy them where they can have the greatest benefit, and work to foster good communication and clear responsibilities for each team member. With this approach, any group of people can, over time, grow into an effective team.

Occasionally luck, or divine providence, brings together a great team. People with strong skills that mesh well together have all the abilities they need to achieve their collective goals. When these great teams happen, they create forces that have great power.

Lee's great team: Lee's great strength rested in his remarkable ability to think many steps ahead and to see strategic opportunities that others could not envision. As mentioned in Chapter 3, Lee almost certainly had strong brain dominance in the upper right quadrant where imaginative, creative, and strategic thinking takes place.

STUART, LEE AND JACKSON

To feed this strategic thinking, Lee needed intelligence on a broad range of battlefield issues. He combined this information with his personal knowledge of the opposing general and his troops, knowledge he had acquired from having worked with many of them before the war. This helped him understand what his adversaries were likely to do before they did it, and he used intelligence about battlefield operations to decide exactly where an attack should happen to have maximum effect.

Lee was remarkably fortunate to have J.E.B. Stuart as his general in charge of the Confederate cavalry. Stuart and his mounted troops could outride and outfight anything the Union forces threw at them for the first half of the war. Stuart was a master at covering large distances quickly and gaining insights into his enemy's strengths and weaknesses along the way. Stuart's excellent information and Lee's ability to see strategic opportunity were a powerful force for devising creative battle plans that played to Confederate strengths.

With a good plan, Lee needed a good implementer. This role fell to Stonewall Jackson at Chancellorsville. Jackson's troops had a well deserved reputation of being able to move faster and fight harder than any infantry in existence in the mid-nineteenth century.

When the team of Lee, Stuart, and Jackson was in place and functioning well, they were largely unstoppable. But interestingly, apart from the team, Lee was not able to succeed nearly as often or as well. For instance, in the Seven-Day Battle to the northwest of Richmond, Jackson and his troops arrived late and exhausted, and the battle was largely a stalemate. And at Gettysburg, Stuart was unable to join Lee until late in the battle and was therefore not able to provide the critical intelligence Lee needed to win. Because Jackson had died before Gettysburg happened, Lee was left without his winning team at the most critical point in the war.

Grant's team: Though Grant did not have quite as famous a team as Lee, he did have an important partnership with William Tecumseh Sherman and Phillip Sheridan. Certainly, a key part of the Vicksburg victory depended on Grant having a strong right-hand man in Sherman.

When Grant was promoted to lead general of the Union army and moved East, he was able to turn the western operation over to Sherman with great faith that he would effectively execute his theater of the war. Grant took Sheridan with him and made him the head of the cavalry for the Union forces in Virginia, a position that paralleled J.E.B Stuart's. In fact, the Lee/Stuart/Jackson team and the Grant/Sheridan/Sherman team can be viewed as having parallel roles. Perhaps one of the many deciding factors in the war's outcome was that the Union team lived through the war—and Jackson and Stuart did not.

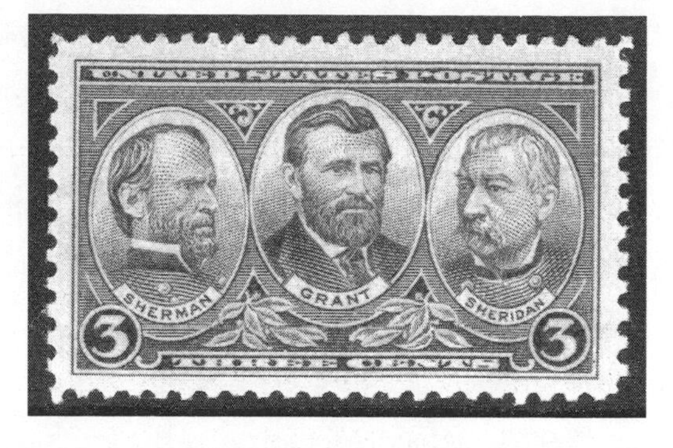

SHERMAN, GRANT AND SHERIDAN

Tom Rath's book *Strengths-Based Leadership* uses volumes of Gallup polls to makes the case that great leaders are generally not worried about balancing their strengths and weaknesses, but rather focused on developing their unique strengths—and that great teams have team members with different skills that together create a balanced team.

Seeing Opportunities and Gaining Momentum

In the Vicksburg campaign, Grant saw that the two Confederate armies in the area were not consolidated and, if they came together, he might be stopped. He was able to first turn his attention to the force at Jackson, Mississippi, defeat it, and then turn to the force at Vicksburg. This strategy was what Sun Tzu meant in *The Art of War* when he wrote, "Your larger force can overwhelm his smaller one. Then go on to the next small enemy group. You can take the one at a time."

Lee's opportunity presented itself when his intelligence report showed that the Union force was much larger than his, but its right flank was not yet organized. Lee sent his best troops under Stonewall Jackson, through the woods and brush, to launch a surprise attack. This sent panic through the Union lines and resulted in Lee's victory.

Both Lee and Grant were open to seeing opportunities and being able to act on them quickly to create momentum. As we have seen in numerous chapters, creating momentum is a powerful tool for motivating and exciting a group to achieve its goal.

Strategic Timing

Both Grant at Vicksburg and Lee at Chancellorsville were able to take the initiative and act when the moment was right. Grant used a distraction to open an opportunity, and Lee was able to identify the time-limited opportunity of the not-yet-organized Union army's right flank.

There is a lot of truth to the saying that timing is everything. The key to taking advantage of timing is to avoid planning in such a detailed way that your plans are locked into a preset timetable. It is better to have the necessary steps of a plan in mind, but have the flexibility to slow down or accelerate those plans, based on external conditions. You need to strike a balance between good planning and the ability to be opportunistic.

The other side of this equation is that neither Grant nor Lee would have been in a position to make the strategically timed move if either lacked ready resources and an overall strategy. Both generals acted in a way that was consistent with Sun Tzu's wisdom that "you can recognize opportunity for victory; you do not create it."

CHAPTER 5

A Compelling Mission: Abraham Lincoln

This is a war to free the master as well as to free the slave. It is a war to break the shackles of ignorance, prejudice, malice, and hate that fetter the souls of you misguided brethren…It is not a war to save the Union alone; it is a war to make the Union worth saving.

These were the words of Lieutenant William Hogart of Artillery Battery B expressed in his paper "A Medal of Honor" in a collection of papers called War Talks in Kansas (1906), and the essence of Lincoln's mission during his presidency.

Making the "Union worth saving," shorthand for freeing the slaves, was the greatest historical contribution President Lincoln made, and the main reason he remains one of the most popular American presidents of all time. Without a mission as significant as human freedom, it is quite possible the war would have ended differently.

The role of slavery in the Civil War was much more complicated than many in the twenty-first century recognize. Though the mission to free the slaves was central to the conflict (and to the outcome of the war), it was not adopted as a goal until about the war's midpoint. The Ordinance of Secession from South Carolina, the first state to declare independence from the United States, contained essentially two arguments: (1) a legal argument that the Revolutionary War established thirteen independent states that voluntarily joined together to create the United States and could therefore leave the Union at any time, and (2) the North had become increasingly hostile towards the institution of slavery and had adopted state laws that effectively nullified the federal Fugitive Slave Act (the law requiring the return of escaped slaves). South Carolina, by seceding in this way, was acknowledging the central role of slavery in the break between the states.

Slavery was inconsistent with American ideals of liberty: Slavery was debated by the Founders of the nation and by every subsequent generation. Then, from the late eighteenth century until the Civil War, two powerful forces began impacting the slavery debate. One force was the growth of the slave economy in the South, due to the invention of the cotton gin in 1790 and the need to increase cotton harvests to meet the demand for cotton production. The other force was the growth of a strong Abolitionist Movement driven largely but not exclusively by Quakers. The tension between these two forces finally erupted into war.

Despite personally believing in emancipation, Lincoln was slow to make human freedom a central issue in the war. For the first half of the war the mission of the North was to preserve the Union. This was a legal abstraction for which people were being asked to fight, endure great hardship, and die—not a compelling mission.

Compare this to what was happening in the South, where most of the combat was taking place. Many of the rank and file soldiers in the Confederate Armies were fighting a war of invasion. Throughout history, defending against an invading army has always been a powerful motivation and mission regardless of the politics involved.

The contrast between missions and motivations during the first eighteen months of the war is one of the reasons the South had so many military successes during that time.

Lincoln was slow to give the Union troops "something worth fighting for" for several reasons. First, he understood the tradeoff between a mission that can be universally accepted but that has no strong purpose or passion, and a mission with real purpose that will not be universally accepted. For example, the Abolitionists had great passion and moral righteousness, but many citizens did not share their zeal for universal freedom. General George McClellan, for instance, was strongly opposed to the emancipation of slaves and lobbied Lincoln hard not to make slavery a reason for the war (see Chapter 3). McClellan even threatened to quit if Lincoln made slavery a central issue, and when Lincoln ignored McClellan's threat, McClellan ran against him in the 1864 presidential campaign. Lincoln had believed for a time that he could not afford the political fallout of emancipation, and there was considerable fallout (such as riots in New York) when he finally took action. But as he came to realize, the war could not have been won by the North without a powerful mission to motivate the great sacrifices that were necessary.

Making the war about human freedom and liberty was the death knell for the Confederate cause. Politically, the end game for the Confederacy had been to gain official recognition by England and/or France that the Confederate States of America were an independent nation. If this had happened, the dynamics of the war would have changed from that of a civil war to that of two nation-states fighting, and the South would have achieved its goal.

As long as the war was officially about preserving the Union and not slavery, the European powers could flirt with recognizing the South as a sovereign nation. Many English nobles liked the Southern idea of a nation ruled by an aristocracy. In the summer of 1863, in fact, a motion was made in the British Parliament to recognize the Confederacy. In the debate, English politician John Bright argued against recognizing the Confederacy in this speech to Parliament:

> *We see that the Government of the United States has for two years past been contending for its life, and we know that it is contending necessarily for human freedom. That Government affords the remarkable example—offered for the first time in the history of the world—of a great Government coming forward as the organized defender of law, freedom, and equity. Surely honor able Gentlemen [those proposing Confederate recognition] cannot be so ill-informed as to say that the revolt of the Southern States is in favor of freedom and equality.*

JOHN BRIGHT

In finally making the war about freedom, Lincoln gave the troops something of real meaning to fight and die for, and effectively closed off any chance that a European power would align itself with the South.

Leadership Insights

ABRAHAM LINCOLN

To be fully effective, an organization needs a clear mission. Why are we engaged in this enterprise? What are we trying to accomplish in the end? Without a clear mission it is not only difficult to motivate people, it is also more likely that individuals and groups within the organization may be working at cross purposes.

The higher the personal risk involved, the clearer and more lofty the mission must be. If, for example, a job has great benefits, wonderful salary, and little pressure or risk of failure, you may not need as noble a cause to attract and retain talent, although it would help. But as the levels of personal risk go up, motivation can be maintained by a noble mission. While some may view it as fluff, a truly effective organization should have a powerful mission statement, make it always visible, and tie everything in its strategic plans back to the mission. Organizations succeed when their mission is fully integrated in what they do. Organizations risk failure when the actions of the organization are not consistent with the expressed mission.

Sun Tzu addressed this in the *Art of War* when he said, "Command your people in a way that gives them a higher shared purpose. You can lead them to death. You can lead them to life."

Another important lesson in this story is that a passionate mission came at a political price. As long as Lincoln went with the weak but universally accepted mission of preserving the Union, he had wide support but not deep support. When he defied his head general and withstood riots in the streets and a fracturing of his political coalition, Lincoln was able to gain the passion that his efforts lacked before. This deeper but less universal support was needed to win the war.

CHAPTER 6

The Power of Progress: Thomas Jackson

Thomas "Stonewall" Jackson was a stern uncompromising general who regularly pushed his troops beyond the bounds of human endurance. He earned the nickname "Stonewall" in the First Battle of Bull Run (Manassas) in the summer of 1861 by not yielding the field while those all around him were being pushed back.

Military students still study his remarkable Valley Campaign, conducted in the spring of 1862. In this three-week campaign up and down the Shenandoah Valley, Jackson marched his troops over 350 miles day and night, tying up and defeating three Union Armies larger than his. While McClellan was concerned with the best supply lines, reinforcements, and planning, Jackson was all about speed and keeping his enemies off guard. The Stonewall Brigade became known as "foot cavalry" for their remarkable ability to cover long distances faster than any other infantry. To achieve this speed, Jackson had his soldiers carry nothing other than food and ammunition—and sometimes just ammunition. When soldiers would fall on the side of the road from exhaustion or hunger, Jackson showed no compassion.

Lee valued Jackson's ability to move his troops. After the hard-fought Seven Day Battle outside Richmond, which took place immediately after the Valley Campaign, Lee sent Jackson on a mission to go around the federal troops and attack their main supply depot at Manassas.

The Stonewall Brigade evaded detection and marched more than 50 miles in two days, won a skirmish as Bristoe Station and plundered and destroyed the supplies at Manassas.

Jackson's soldiers, who by anyone's standard should have been exhausted, went head to head with the Iron Brigade at Brawner's Farm and directly into the front lines of the Second Battle of Bull Run (Manassas) the next day. Joined by the rest of the Army of Northern Virginia, Jackson's Brigade and some of Longstreet's forces fiercely fought some of the best units of the Union Army and, at the end of the second day, drove the Union forces into retreat.

The very next day Jackson and the famous Stonewall Brigade, along

Desolate landscape in Fairfax County.

with J.E.B. Stuart's cavalry, were in hot pursuit of the retreating Union army. In Centreville, on their way to the Battle of Oxhill, the largest Civil War battle in Fairfax County, Virginia, the troops stopped by the side of the road. According to John E. Cooke, one of Stuart's cavalry,

> *The scene at this moment was interesting. The men of the Stonewall Brigade and their comrades were lying on the side of the road hungry and exhausted. They had not seen their [supply] wagons since they left the Rappahannock, and the rations secured at Manassas were long since exhausted. Green corn and unripe apples had for several days been their sustenance, and now they were in a country which did not afford even these. The hungry men saw on every side bleak fields and forests, with scarce a roof visible in the entire landscape; and thus famished and worn out, they were lying down awaiting the order to advance and attack. There was no ill-humor visible; on the contrary, jests and laughter greeted the least object calculated to excite them. And then the leader [Jackson] who had nearly marched and fought them to death rode by, they saluted him with tumultuous cheers.*

CONFEDERATE ARMY CROSSING AT WHITE'S FORD.

Five days later, these same soldiers, without regular food rations, in threadbare clothes and worn-out shoes, marched past Temple Hall Farm and splashed across the Potomac River at White's Ford north of Leesburg, entering Maryland with high spirits, singing songs.

THOMAS JACKSON

Leadership Insights

No one would dispute that Stonewall Jackson was a great leader. He was able to repeatedly get his troops to do superhuman actions. They could stand up to the most fiery attacks of the war, never caving in. They could march day and night at a speed and covering a distance that most would think impossible. And as eyewitness John E. Cooke has shown, even after insufficient sleep and food and days of long marches and pitched battles these troops had great spirit.

And yet, Jackson showed no compassion for his troops and little interest in making their lives better. His outfit would have never made it onto any of today's popular "100 Best Places to Work" lists. By any objective standard, the Stonewall Brigade would have ranked as one of the worst places to be during the Civil War. So how can you have the worst conditions and the highest spirits and willingness to push on?

In the January–February 2010 issue of Harvard Business Review, Teresa Amabile and Steve Kramer suggest an answer. Amabile and Kramer, reporting on a study about motivating people, found that progress—not compensation or benefits—is what significantly impacts motivation. When people feel they are making headway and achieving goals, they are most motivated to do more.

Consider this in the context of Jackson and his soldiers. Before Jackson earned the name "Stonewall" at the First Battle of Bull Run (Manassas), his troops used to call their moody and secretive commander "Crazy Tom Jackson." After he led them to fame in the Valley Campaign, where they became known for being the best fighters in the war, they followed him anywhere.

As a leader you need to create progress and foster recognition of success and progress in your group. Then your people, too, will follow you anywhere.

CHAPTER 7

Professionalism and Organizational Roles: Charles Stone

Shortly after midnight on February 9, 1862, Brigadier General Charles P. Stone was walking down the dark streets of Washington on his way home. He had spent the evening with other senior officers at the Willard Hotel reviewing newly compiled maps of the South and discussing combat strategies. For General Stone, who was a West Point-educated engineer, a veteran of the Mexican War, and a trained surveyor, studying maps and discussing the condition and use of various rail lines must have been an enjoyable way to spend an evening. Stone had spent two years studying the militaries of Europe and was respected and admired by most of his peers.

In the first days of the War, Stone had been a rising star. He volunteered to enter the Army for a second career shortly before the war broke out, and his old commander, General Winfield Scott, put Stone in charge of security for the nation's capital as Washington got ready for president-elect Abraham Lincoln's arrival. Then Stone took command of the Union forces stationed along the Maryland side of the Potomac River, north of Washington. All was fine until October 1861, when three events—a grilling by the newly formed U.S. Congress Joint Committee on the Conduct of the War, the Battle of Ball's Bluff, and the death of Senator Col. Edward D. Baker at Ball's Bluff—had put Stone under a cloud. Now, four months later, the evening with senior officers had given him a slight respite from that darkness.

GEORGE SYKES

But as Stone approached his house, he saw an officer pacing in front of his door. It was his old comrade George Sykes, also a brigadier general now in command of the City Guard. The two had served together in the Mexican War.

"I have the most disagreeable duty to perform that I ever had," Sykes said. "It is to arrest you."

Shocked, Stone asked what the charges were. Sykes did not know, but could only say that he was being sent to Fort Lafayette Prison in New York on the orders of General George McClellan.

"Why, Fort Lafayette is where they send secessionists!" Stone said. "This is astonishing. They are now sending there me, who has been as true a soldier to the government as any in service."

FORT LAFAYETTE

The next afternoon, a

lieutenant and two policemen escorted General Stone, by train, to prison. In a bizarre turn of events, there was a problem with their tickets upon arriving in Philadelphia. Stone, always the gentleman, personally purchased the tickets for himself and his guards so they could continue on their journey to his jail cell.

News of Stone's arrest traveled fast, and many officers wrote letters on his behalf. "If he is a traitor I am a traitor, and we are all traitors," his old commander General Winfield Scott said.

Stone spent over six months in prison without any knowledge of the charges against him, despite his vigorous letter-writing campaign to find out. He was finally released without explanation or apology after Senator James McDougall, aware of Stone's plight and trying to force his release, attached a section onto a bill on military pay that said an arrested officer must be released if there were no charges brought within eight days and a trial within thirty days.

It took Stone another six months before he was able to appear before the Joint Committee of Congress, learn the accusations against him, and to clear his name. This is what he learned: he had been unfairly blamed for Senator Col. Edward Baker's death in battle. This is how events unfolded:

On October 20, 1861, Stone had received the following orders:

> *Gen. McClellan desires me to inform you that Gen. McCall occupied Dranesville yesterday and is still there. Will send out heavy reconnaissances today in all directions from that point. The general desires that you keep a good lookout upon Leesburg, to see if this movement has the effect to drive them away. Perhaps a slight demonstration*

on your part would have the effect to move them.

Stone's understanding of these orders was that he should send a party across the river to see if Confederates were on the move around Leesburg. If Stone needed help, General McCall's troops were not far away and moving in the direction of Leesburg. Stone sent troops across the river to Virginia without incident, and informed McClellan by telegraph of this news. McClellan responded with congratulations.

The next day, however, did not go well for the Union. Ball's Bluff, an area of Virginia shoreline on the Potomac River, has an eighty-foot drop-off from the fields and forests above to the river below. The Union scouting party at this point saw haystacks in the distance that they mistook for tents of a confederate camp, and requested backup. All day, Union troops trickled across the Potomac on several small boats. They even carried across three pieces of artillery that they tugged up the narrow trail that winds up the bank. Knowing how difficult it was to have a large crossing at Balls Bluff, Stone took another group of his command and crossed at Edwards Ferry, a few miles away, and tried to meet up with the rest of his command at Balls Bluff.

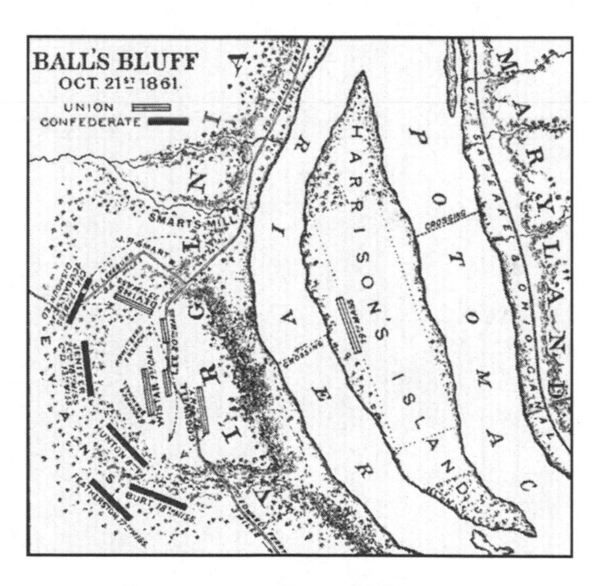

BATTLE OF BALL'S BLUFF

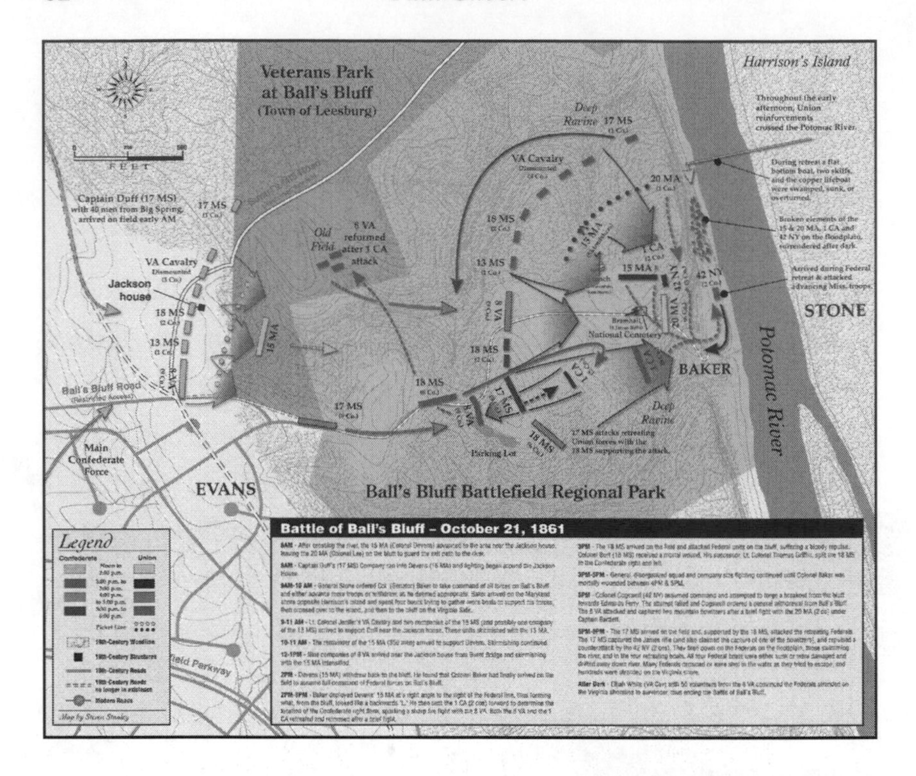

Stopped by Confederate forces, Stone was unable to reinforce his group on the bluffs, where Col. Edward Baker was the ranking officer. Baker was a longtime personal friend of Abraham Lincoln and a former U.S. Senator from California, but he'd had little military training. Resisting the advice of the other officers, Baker set up the Union lines in an open field with their backs to the bluffs. Confederate forces, under cover of the forest, pushed in from three sides and eventually drove the Union troops right off the cliff. Roughly half the 2,000-soldier Union force at Ball's Bluff was killed, wounded, or captured. Among the

Death of Col. Baker

dead was Col. Baker.

Members of Congress, not wanting to believe that their departed friend, the former Senator, could have made mistakes, cast their blame on Stone. In their investigation two junior officers, Captain Brady and Major Dimmick, testified that Stone had allowed some packages to go across the border, implying that he was a traitor. Brady had been upset that Stone had not granted him leave to attend to personal business; we do not know why Dimmick was willing to imply disloyalty with no solid proof. The Committee also heard from an informant that the Confederate officers considered Stone a gentleman. That was all they needed to arrest him. (Since Stone had gone to West Point and fought in the Mexican War, it is highly likely that some of the Confederate officers in the area knew him personally, as was common throughout the Civil War.)

McClellan had initially reported that Stone had done nothing wrong in the execution of his duties on October 21, 1861, and that Baker was at fault. But when Stone went before the Joint Committee on the War, he was under orders from McClellan not to tell Congress anything about his orders or actions. Being the good soldier, Stone did not impress the angry members of Congress when he gave only vague answers to their questions. When Secretary of War Edward Stanton, under pressure from members of Congress, ordered Stone's arrest, McClellan did not defend the person he knew as being innocent.

EDWARD BAKER

Stone's reputation as being both loyal and competent was among the best of any officer in the Union Army. For example, when Stone was initially assigned the job of organizing the defenses of Washington in January 1861, he inspected all the volunteer militia units in the city and found that the best-armed unit, the National Rifles Company under the command of Captain Schaeffer, was in fact dominated by Secessionists. Stone planted a spy in the unit and learned they were planning to take over the Federal Department of Treasury as part of a planned coup before Lincoln was sworn in.

Stone wrote an article in 1887 ("Washington on the Eve of the War") recounting the story of how he foiled the attempted coup. Stone had ordered this secessionist company to turn into the armory the cannons, sabers, and revolvers they had been issued because these weapons were not needed for a company of riflemen. Captain Schaeffer protested.

> *Before he had time to speak [Stone wrote]*
> *I informed him that I had a commission*
> *of Major for his name. He was much pleased,*
> *and said: 'Yes, I heard that I had been appointed.'*
> *I then handed him a slip of paper on which*
> *I had written out the form of oath which the*
> *old law required to be taken by officers, that*
> *law never had been repealed, and I said to him:*
> *'Here is the form of oath you are to take. You*
> *will find a justice of the peace on the next*
> *floor. Please qualify, sign the form in duplicate,*
> *and bring both to me. One will be filed with*
> *your letter of acceptance, the other will be*
> *filed in the clerk's office of the Circuit Court*
> *of the District.' He took the paper with a*

sober look, and stood near my table several minutes looking at the form of oath and turned the paper over, while I, apparently very busy with my papers, was observing him closely. I then said:

'Ah, Schaeffer, have you already taken the oath?'

'No,' said he.

'Well, please be quick about it, as I have no time to spare.'

He hesitated, and said slowly:

'In ordinary times I would not mind taking it, but in these times--'

'Ah!' Said I, 'you decline to accept your commission of major. Very well!!' And I returned his commission to the drawer and locked it in.

'Oh no,' said Schaeffer, 'I want the commission.'

'But, sir, you cannot have it. Do you suppose that, in these times, which are not, as you say, ordinary times, I would think of delivering a commission of field-officer to a man who hesitates about taking the oath of office? Do you think that the government of the United States is stupid enough to allow a man to march armed men about the federal district under its authority, when that man hesitates to take the simple oath of office? No, sir, you cannot have this commission; and more than that, I now inform you that

> *you hold no office in the District of Columbia volunteers.'*
> *'Yes, I do; I am captain, and have my commission as such, signed by the President and delivered to me by the major-general.'*
> *'I am aware that such a paper was delivered to you, but you failed legally to accept it.'*
> *'I wrote a letter of acceptance to the adjutant-general, and forwarded it through the major-general.'*
> *'Yes, I am aware that you did; but I know also that you failed to enclose in that letter, according to law, the form of oath required to accompany all letters of acceptance...'*
> *So Captain Schaeffer left the 'National Rifles,' and with him left the secession members of that company."*

Stone's reputation as a fine leader was so good that after he was released from prison, General Joseph Hooker, recently named Commander of the Army of the Potomac, requested that Stone become his Chief of Staff. This request was turned down by Secretary Stanton, since it would have confirmed Stanton's poor judgment in the arrest and imprisonment of Charles Stone.

Stone never received a significant post again, and resigned his commission shortly before the end of the war. After the war, General George Sherman helped Stone get a job as a general in the Egyptian Army where he served for a number of years.

In a final irony, Stone's last job was that of Chief Engineer of the foundation and base for the Statue of Liberty, built within sight of the prison where he had been held without trial or charges.

Leadership Insights

There are many lessons, both positive and negative, in this story. On the positive side, Charles Stone conducted himself with great dignity throughout a horrible ordeal that he did not deserve. And because of his deep professionalism, he won respect and assistance from commanders like Joseph Hooker and George Sherman who could see that not only was Stone very competent, but he could also handle tremendous stress.

Much of Stone's problems came from a governance board (the Joint Committee on the War) that was both fearful of how the war was going and unclear about the proper divide between governance and management. Also, senior management from Secretary Stanton and General McClellan did not demonstrate the courage to do their job by standing up for a wrongly accused employee.

Governance is a concept that is not well understood by many. The governance role is that of oversight and policy. Almost every organization has this role, which is assigned to a Board of Directors or elected bodies. The members of these bodies provide financial oversight, including audit committees, and regularly review the financial report of the organization. They create policies and work with senior management to set goals and strategic plans. In many organizations, they also approve annual budgets, the nerve system of any organization. In most cases, the governance board hires the organization's chief executive and sets this executive's compensation—making the chief executive their sole employee. The Board of Directors can hire, fire, and manage this person, but have no role other than to set policy related to any other employees in the organization. The other employees report through a chain of command up to the chief executive. The executive and the management team are responsible for the management of the organization and the execution of the strategic goals and policies set by the governance board.

CHARLES STONE

This difference between governance roles and responsibilities and management roles has challenged many organizations. Because most successful people are doers, the role of governance is not always easy or natural. As a result, governance boards sometimes slip intoactions that go beyond their mandate. In Stone's case, the two junior officers who cast vague aspersions that Stone had been too friendly with the enemy played right into the Joint Committee's desire to micromanage.

Any organization of significant size is more than likely to contain some employees with ulterior motives that will lead them into mischief if given the chance.

These factors could have been muted if either Secretary of War Stanton, or Stone's commander, General McClellan, had done their jobs and not allowed the Joint Committee to indulge their interest in punishing someone who did not work directly for them. If McClellan had thought that Stone acted wrongly, he could have transferred, demoted, or court-martialed Stone himself. And if he thought Stone was innocent, he should have stood up for his employee. Either way, he should never have bent to the will of those in Congress who had no authority to act in this matter.

A large part of this problem was with McClellan. One of the most important responsibilities for any chief executive is to make sure the governance board has the best possible information to do its job. In modern organizations, this can mean financial information that is not only accurate but accessible, so that Board members can easily understand the information and identify patterns, trends, and mission-related updates of the goals and strategic initiatives of the organization. McClellan did just the opposite and ordered Stone to give the Joint Committee no information about his orders, thereby obscuring vital context. McClellan had significant insecurities, and he was probably worried that he would become Congress' target if Congress saw that he had suggested some kind of action in his orders.

One of the best thinkers on why governance boards sometimes slip beyond their mandate and inject themselves in management issues is Hildy Gottlieb (www.creatingthefuture.org), a consultant focused on helping the nonprofit sector. In her paper "Why Boards Micro-Manage" (help4nonprofits.com), she identifies six underlying problems:

> *1. The board has no clear sense of its role in the organization, and no system to guide that role. Board members think this is what they should be doing.*
>
> *2. The board has no policies or procedures delineating appro priate roles for staff vs. the board.*
>
> *3. Most people have no experience in "leading." Our real-life experience is mostly doing.*
>
> *4. Board members are recruited to perform tasks, not to lead.*
>
> *5. Remnants of Crisis: During significant organizational crises,*

> *sometimes a board needs to play a more active role and, after such a crisis, some boards may let the memory of that crisis influence their actions long after the situation has passed.*
>
> *6. Fear: Boards fear that if they don't do "it," no one else will. Fear that the organization will fail. Fear about money, about bad press. When boards behave badly, they are usually concerned about the health and safety of the organization.*

One can see these points play out in the case of the Joint Committee on the War: Committee members might not have had clearly defined roles, but they clearly were in the midst of a crisis, with a war that was going badly, and they clearly were acting out of fear.

Gottlieb's suggested solution is not just to focus on the problem of micromanagement, but to see micromanagement as a symptom of the larger issues listed above. Her solution is "one part compassion, and one part wisdom."

The compassion part is to realize that when boards micromanage, they are not intentionally creating problems. Gottlieb notes, "Board Members micro-manage because they care, they are scared, and they don't know what else to do." Assuming the best intentions of others is always a good starting point to resolve issues.

The wisdom portion of her solution is an understanding that it is hard, if not impossible, to achieve a negative—and "stopping micromanagement" is a negative statement. The positive goal that can be achieved is to engage the board actively in governance. If the board is actively engaged in the right things, it is much less likely to drift outside its important role. Providing excellent information on how the overall organization is doing and engaging the board in thoughtful discussions about strategic direction and goals are two ways to help a board do its job well.

Sarbanes-Oxley legislation, put in place in 2002 as a reaction to the financial misdeeds of Enron and WorldCom, put a much greater focus on the oversight role of governance boards of public companies. The main provisions of this bill have relevance to this discussion of micromanagement and proper governance, namely:

- Chief executives and financial officers are held responsible for their companies' financial reports.
- Executive officers and directors may not solicit or accept loans from their companies.
- Insider trades are reported more quickly.
- Insider trades are prohibited during pension-fund blackout periods.
- Disclosure of executive compensation and profits is mandatory.
- Internal audits and review and certification of audits by outside auditors are mandatory.
- There will be criminal and civil penalties for securities violations.
- There will be longer jail sentences and larger fines for executives who intentionally misstate financial statements.
- Audit firms may no longer provide actuarial, legal, or consulting services to firms they audit.
- Publicly traded companies must establish internal financial controls and have those controls audited annually.

Sarbanes-Oxley legislation emerged as a response to the concern that the boards of some public companies were not adequately focused on the important role of a governance board in financial oversight. This bill more clearly defined the fiduciary responsibility of boards of public companies and in the process helped better define this element of governance.

But governance goes beyond the green eyeshade elements of the legislation. Governance is perhaps most important as a role in making sure the organization has a mission and goals and is moving towards those goals. This is a potentially tricky area because some people are very detail focused and can have a difficult time seeing and focusing on the big picture. But governance is very much a big picture role. The role of good governance in any organization is vital.

Anyone who serves on a governance board or in a management role must understand the difference in responsibilities for these areas, and how they intersect to make an effective organization with good decision making at all levels.

The dynamics of this relationship are very similar, whether it is the Congress and Army, a city council and city government, a nonprofit, or a corporation.

Robert C. Pozen, a senior lecturer at Harvard Business School and financial industry expert, addressed the need to make reforms beyond what Sarbanes-Oxley provided when he wrote "The Case for Professional Board," published in the December 2010 Harvard Business Review. Pozen believes organizations would be better off with smaller boards that can act more effectively as decision-making bodies. He cites Citigroup, which had eighteen Board Members, as an example of diluting personal responsibility for the organization. Pozen suggests an optimum number of around seven board members. He also makes a case for board members who devote more time to understanding the fundamentals of the organization to help themselves do a better job of governance.

There probably is no one optimal profile of an effective governance board. While wisdom suggests that group dynamics work better if the group remains small, often the number of board members is set by law, politics, or other dynamics that are not easily changed.

Many nonprofit boards need a higher number of board members to facilitate the all-important role of fundraising. The primary challenge for any governance board, then, is to focus on how best to help the organization achieve its strategic goals in a positive and productive way. If the focus stays on strategy and oversight, the organization will benefit.

One of the great legacies of Stone's story is that it affected the organizational culture of Union commanders. By allowing Congress to unjustly punish an officer who took initiative in executing the battle plan and lost, it fostered a tendency of many Union officers to shy away from engaging the enemy.

It was not until almost two years after Ball's Bluff that the Union was able to put commanders in place, first Hooker and finally Grant, who were willing to aggressively fight the war. It might be interesting to speculate on how the Civil War would have been different if Union commanders knew they would be supported even if they lost a battle. This could have reduced the length of the war by years.

CHAPTER 8

Decisive Leadership: J.E.B. Stuart

One of the most romanticized Civil War leaders was J.E.B. Stuart, the general in charge of the Confederate cavalry under Robert E. Lee. The South used its cavalry to much greater effect than did the North (until Phil Sheridan applied their example late in the war). The North assigned small groups of cavalry to infantry units, whereas the South viewed cavalry as an independent branch of the army, used both as an intelligence-gathering tool and a rapid deployment force. These were roles that Stuart perfected.

With his dapper uniform, ostrich-feathered hat, red-lined cape, and his insistence about being at the front lines of any engagement, Stuart won a reputation as the gallant cavalier. (An interesting foot-note: at the same time Stuart was commanding Confederate cavalry, his father-in-law, General Cooke, was the senior commander of the Union cavalry.)

In the summer of 1862, McClellan's army of more than 100,000 troops was positioned to crush Richmond and end the war. As Lee's scouts examined the strength of the Union forces, they found it hard to get a good read on the right flank. Lee ordered Stuart to take 1,200 mounted soldiers and investigate McClellan's right flank for potential weaknesses. With this assignment, Stuart cemented his place in history by leading one of the most daring operations of the war.

To avoid detection, the Confederate cavalry left Richmond on June 12, in the middle of the night. They fought and captured a number of Union soldiers and saw that there was a potential opportunity for a larger action on the right flank in the future. At that point, they could have turned around and tried to make their way back to Richmond, but that is not what happened. Instead, Stuart opted for a daring ride around the entire Union army.

Captain John E. Cooke, an aide to Stuart, recalled the trajectory of the decision, which happened after they had gathered the needed intelligence and captured a depot with a great deal of supplies:

> *Stuart had decided upon his course with that rapidity, good judgment, and decision, which were the real secret of his splendid efficiency as a leader of cavalry, in which capacity I believe that he has never been surpassed… . He was now in the very heart of the enemy's citadel, with enormous masses upon every side. He had driven in their advance force, passed within sight of the white tents of General McClellan's headquarters, burned their camps, and ascertained all that he wished. How was he to return? He could not cross the Pamunkey, and make the circuit back; he had no pontoons. He could not return over the*

> *route by which he had advanced. The alarm had been given and an overpowering force of infantry, cavalry, and artillery had been rapidly moved in that direction to intercept the daring raiders... He must find some other loophole of escape.*

The plan that unfolded was one of the most remarkable cavalry actions of the war. Stuart and his 1,200 soldiers rode day and night, covering more than 150 miles in a little more than two days, riding completely around and through the mass of McClellan's army. Along the way, they cut supply and communications lines, captured and destroyed large stockpiles of supplies, and fought numerous small engagements with surprised Union forces. Indeed, the cavalry slept in their saddles: Captain Cooke wrote about holding General Stuart upright in the saddle so he could sleep while they rode through the night. At every minute of this two-and-a-half-day odyssey they

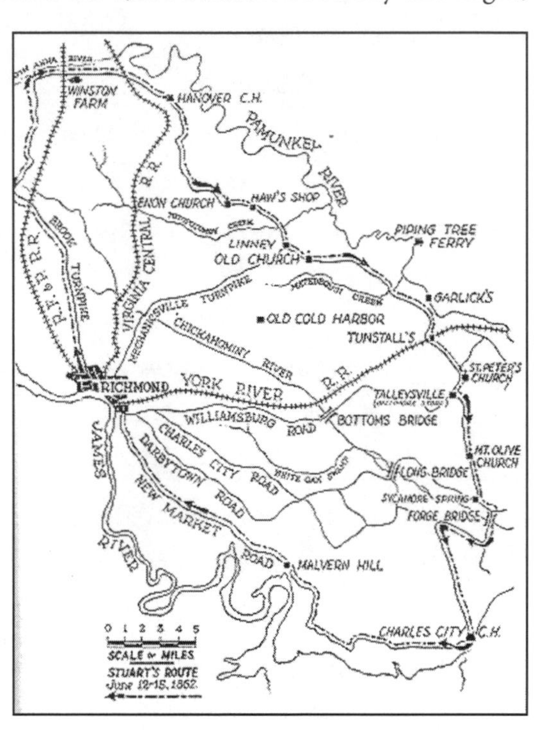

STUART'S RIDE AROUND MCLELLAN

didn't know if they would find an overwhelming force around the next bend in the road.

On the morning of June 15, 1862, when they were within a few miles of the Confederate lines and safety, Stuart's army came to the ford in the Chickahominy River, intending to cross but finding the river swollen and impassable.

Colonel William H.F. Lee was one of the first to arrive. "I think we are caught," he said.

They all knew the Union forces were on their heels and would be there soon.

When Stuart arrived, he moved the troops downstream to where a bridge had been. Only the stone abutments on either side remained, and between them flowed 30–40 feet of fast-moving water.

A few years later, Captain Cooke wrote this in his book, *Wearing of the Gray*:

> *Stuart gave his personal supervision to the work, he and his staff laboring with the men. A skiff was procured; this was affixed by a rope to a tree, in the mid-current just above the abutments, and thus a movable pier was secured in the middle of the stream. An old barn was then hastily torn to pieces and robbed of its timbers; these were stretched down to the boat, and up to the opposite abutment, and a foot-bridge was thus ready. Large numbers of the men immediately unsaddled their horses, took their equipment over, and then returned, drove or rode their*

> *horses into the stream, and swam them over. In this manner a considerable number crossed; but the process was much too slow. There, besides, was the artillery, which Stuart had no intention of leaving. A regular bridge must be built with out a moment's delay, and to this work Stuart now applied himself with ardor.*

The group continued to deconstruct the barn and build a bridge capable of transporting the artillery over.

> *Stuart worked with the men, and as the planks thundered down, and the bridge steadily advanced, the gay voice of the General was heard humming a song. He was singing carelessly, although at every instant an overpowering force of enemy was looking for them.*

Stuart was able to complete the bridge and move his entire force, including the artillery, to safety—and destroy the bridge behind him. As the rear of the Confederate forces moved on towards their own lines, the Union cavalry arrived in time to shoot at them from the banks of the river, where Stuart and his troops had worked on the barn-bridge moments earlier.

When Stuart arrived in Richmond that morning with fresh intelligence, additional supplies, and the story of this "Mission Impossible," it created a great sensation.

J.E.B. STUART

Leadership Insights

J.E.B. Stuart had many great leadership characteristics. He understood his adversaries and the skills of his own group and was able to take advantage of his and his army's strengths. He knew his group had a good knowledge of the area and the ability to move quickly. His adversaries were not as familiar with the area, and would be surprised by his actions and slow to respond. With this knowledge and understanding, he won the day.

It is not always easy to see and use your strengths when you are completely outnumbered (1200 Confederates riding around and through 100,000 Union troops). Even with 100 to 1 against him, he was able to leverage the strengths of his group.

Stuart exhibited decisive leadership, which is the ability of leaders to change directions based on new information, even taking unconventional or unprecedented actions if circumstances call for them. By this standard, Stuart was extremely decisive. He had scouts in all directions, assessing the situation and feeding that information back to him. He took the information and decided to fight, circumvent, or even fabricate a bridge if the circumstances called for it.

In a 2008 study on the effect of decisive and indecisive leaders on organizations, Junichiro Ishiad of Osaka University in Japan found that what a leader did with information had a great influence on how good the organization was at acquiring information. If leaders played it safe by maintaining the status quo, then the individuals in the organization did not stretch themselves to gain new information about the market and were generally less motivated. When the leadership was viewed as willing to take bold steps, the rest of the organization did a better job of obtaining and processing information.

Another characteristic made Stuart a great leader: rather than focusing his energy and attention on problems that could not be changed, he focused narrowly on the opportunity. We can see this best in the story about the bridge. When others' assessment of the river that could not be forded was that "all was lost," Stuart turned his focus on the stone abutments that had once held a bridge and on the materials at hand, which included a small boat and a barn close to the site. By looking for opportunity, however difficult, he was able to pull off a remarkable feat and safely convey his whole group to the river's opposite bank.

He worked alongside the other men in constructing the bridge and hummed while he worked, allowing him to focus the energy of the group on the high-priority work, keep morale high in a tense situation, and oversee that the work was being done in the most effective way.

Surprise was a great contributor to the success of the endeavor. Because they had a 100,000-person force on the doorsteps of Richmond, the Union forces were not expecting an attack, and certainly never considered that the Confederate cavalry would try to ride around and through their entire army. This bold strategy would have been approved by Sun Tzu, who wrote, "You must use surprise for a successful escape. Surprise is as infinite as the weather and land. Surprise is as inexhaustible as the flow of a river."

By pulling off such a bold move, Stuart secured his reputation as perhaps the best cavalry commander in the war. Consequently, his force would follow him anywhere and always assume victory. This served him very well until another battle outside Richmond, where he was killed in a conflict with the forces of Phil Sheridan.

CHAPTER 9

The Power of Personality: Phillip Sheridan

Lieutenant Benson of New York's 19th Corps of the 128th Regiment would have been exhausted if he weren't so pumped up with adrenaline. The Union Army of the Shenandoah had been in retreat since 5:00 A.M. on October 19, 1864, after the Confederates had attacked its camp on the north side of Cedar Creek.

Now it was early afternoon and Union army had been pushed back for miles towards Winchester, Virginia. Benson and his group were better prepared than most for the attack, because they had been getting ready early for a scouting mission that in fact never happened. Much of the army was just starting the day, cooking some coffee and bacon, and they were not ready for combat.

The surprise attack was a demoralizing rout for the Union. In response, disorganized groups of soldiers walked north towards the base they had left a few weeks ago in Winchester. The army had been pushed out of its camp so quickly that they had lost all their artillery to the enemy and most of the equipment and supplies that could not be taken with them in their hasty retreat.

General Phil Sheridan had led this army to victory twice in the previous month, battling Southerners led by General Jubal Early. The victories were such a success that the Union felt Early's army in the Shenandoah Valley was nearly defeated. Thus, Sheridan had been called to Washington to meet with Secretary of War Stanton and General Halleck to help plan the next steps in the war. Sheridan had made his meetings in Washington brief and he set out for Winchester the night before the Confederates launched their surprise attack.

As he rode toward Cedar Creek, Sheridan began to realize what was happening that morning in the Union camp. At first, he heard the cannons in the distance, then sustained gunfire, then soldiers fleeing the front, who could only say that all was lost.

Faced with this scene, Sheridan wrote in his personal memoirs,

> *My first thought was to stop the army in the suburbs of Winchester as it came back, form a new line, and fight there; but as the situation was more maturely considered a better conception prevailed. I was sure the troops had confidence in me, for theretofore we had been successful; and as at other times they had seen me present at the slightest sign of trouble or distress, I felt that I ought to try now to restore their broken ranks, or, failing that, to share their fate because of what they had done hitherto.*

Meanwhile, Lieutenant Benson was trying again to get the New Yorkers into battle formation. In his memoirs, Sheridan wrote about how his arrival was met with jubilation:

> *... loud cheering was heard to the left of our line. We were not kept long in suspense as to its cause. Sheridan had arrived, mounted on a powerful black horse, he rode at great speed down the front of our line, waving his hat and calling out words of encouragement to our men... Passing down his lines he produced, as he ever did, an enthusiasm in all the men, and a new confidence of success.*

Acting on his plan, Sheridan sent his cavalry out to round up the soldiers who were wandering across the fields, and every mounted officer

PAINTING OF SHERIDAN'S RIDE

he met he sent out to the right and left to spread the word that he was back and that they would retake their camp at Cedar Creek that day.

His presence was a key factor in getting most of the army assembled and in formation.

> *Major Forsyth now suggested that it would be well to ride along the line of battle before the enemy assailed us, for although the troops had learned of my return, but a few of them had seen me. Following his suggestion I started in behind the men, but when a few paces had been taken I crossed to the front and, hat in hand, passed along the entire length of the infantry line; and it is from this circumstance that many of the officers and men who then received me with such heartiness have since supposed that that was my first appearance on the field.*

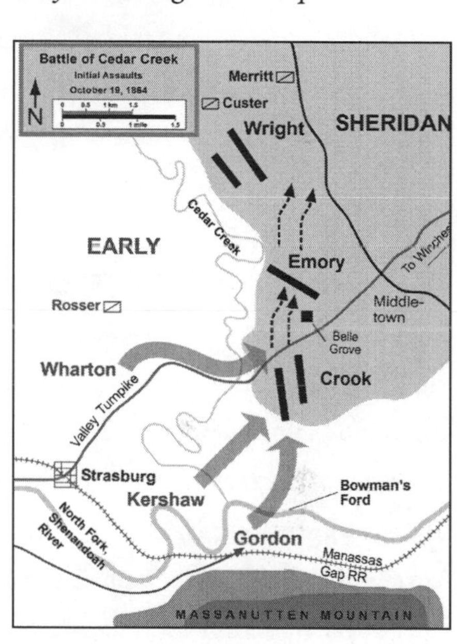

BATTLE OF CEDAR CREEK

With their newfound energy and confidence, the Army of Shenandoah pushed forward and regained its camp and all of the artillery—their own and the enemy's. They pushed on until night fall. The Southern army in the Shenandoah Valley was never again a significant force. Reflecting on this historic moment, Sheridan recalled,

> *I already knew that even in the ordinary condition of mind enthusiasm is a potent element with soldiers, but what I saw that day convinced me that if it can be excited from a state of despondency its power is almost irresistible.*

This battle on October 19, 1864, was largely credited with winning President Abraham Lincoln's second-term election, which had been in significant doubt just weeks before. For this victory, Sheridan was promoted to Major General.

Strangely enough, Sheridan was a very unlikely hero and leader. The son of working-class Irish immigrants who had moved first to New York and then to Ohio, he had gone to West Point but graduated near the bottom of his class and was suspended for a year for fighting. Lincoln had described Sheridan as "a chunky little chap, with a long body, short legs, not enough neck to hang him, and such long arms that if his ankles itch he can scratch them without stooping."

Sheridan served the first two-thirds of the war in relative obscurity, but both General Halleck and Grant saw the tremendous potential in him and put him in the right leadership positions. Grant said,

No man ever had such a faculty of finding out things as Sheridan, or of knowing all about the enemy. He was always the best-informed man in his command as to the enemy. Then he had that magnetic quality of swaying men which I wish I had—a rare quality in a general.

Leadership Insights

From all accounts, Phil Sheridan had charisma, that quality of personality that inspires and motivates all those around. Until recently, charisma seemed like one of those qualities one can only aspire to.

Now we may be on the verge of unlocking the workings of this magnetic trait. Professor Alex "Sandy" Pentland of the MIT Human Dynamics Lab, and author of Honest Signals, is leading research into charisma and other nonverbal social signaling. Through measuring nonverbal cues like gestures, tone, expression, and other characteristics, Pentland's researchers can predict with a high degree of accuracy who will win business deals or succeed with salary negotiations. Energetic and positive people who spend more face-to-face time with those with whom they're dealing have a high degree of success in swaying others to their point of view and making those around them more positive and energetic at the same time. Through becoming aware of social signals (and which ones have a positive effect on others), people can learn to be more charismatic and elicit the best in others.

PHILLIP SHERIDAN

Sheridan's behavior showed that he was very honest. He initially won the admiration of General Halleck when he cleaned up corruption in the quartermaster's office. He held his staff to high standards, and when someone did not meet the performance standards Sheridan had set, he removed them from their position of authority. These traits of honesty and high standards coupled with Sheridan's high energy and sociable demeanor made Sheridan a leader people trusted and wanted to follow.

In Honest Signals, Pentland writes that when people take a leadership role they "display a combination of attention, interest, and great focus in thought and purpose." This leads to high activity and energy levels and a consistent emphasis and rhythm to their speech. Humans are hardwired to respond to these signals, and so it is easy for one person to sway large groups who are exposed to the signals such leaders send out. This is clearly what happened in the fields south of Winchester on that October afternoon, as Sheridan rode down the army's line shouting to the troops and waving his hat in the air.

And there was a "domino" effect: this dramatic victory was believed to have secured Lincoln's second term in office, which in turn secured Union victory in the war. Had Lincoln not won, his opponent, former general George McClellan, likely would have negotiated an end to the war that would have legitimized the Confederacy. This would have vindicated McClellan's belief that the war was un-winnable, based on his lack of meaningful success as the commander.

CHAPTER 10

The Role of Training: John Gibbon

Bullets flew through the air as thick as hail and shells burst overhead one mid-September morning in a Maryland cornfield. The Iron Brigade, a group of "Westerners" from Indiana and Wisconsin, who developed a well-deserved reputation as one of the toughest fighting units in the Union army, was holding its ground in the most horrific single day of battle in the war and the bloodiest day in American history.

As Major Rufus Dawes recalled in "On the Right at Antietam" published in *Sketches of War History* edited by Robert Hunter in 1890,

> *Shells burst around us, the fragments tearing up the ground, and grape shot whistled through the corn above us. Lieutenant Bode, of Company F, was instantly killed by a piece of shell, and Lieutenant John Ticknor was badly wounded. A man now came running to me through the corn. He said: 'Major, Colonel Bragg wants to see you quick*

> *at the turnpike.' I ran to the fence just in time to hear Bragg say: 'Major, I am shot; take command,' before he fell to the ground… I felt a great sense of responsibility when thrown thus suddenly in command of the regiment in the face of a terrible battle.*

Moments later, Major Dawes noticed Brigadier General John Gibbon, a trained artillery officer and Commander of the Iron Brigade and Artillery Battery B. Battery B was holding the flank of the Union forces, but cannoneers were falling fast in the hail of bullets. Gibbon, who had served with Battery B prior to the war, dismounted from his horse and began operating the cannons as a gunner to keep the Confederates from overtaking their position. Soon, Gibbon was "grimed" with powder smoke from operating one cannon almost singlehandedly.

A few minutes later, Gibbon ordered Dawes' regiment to help protect the cannons. Lieutenant William Hogart in his article "A Medal of Honor" in the 1906 publication *War Talks in Kansas*, recalled the order to go into action:

> *No chariot ever raced for gain or glory, no fire patrol every rushed through fire and smoke to the rescue of life or the protection of property, more gallantly than did Battery B to save the right of the Army of the Potomac at Antietam…Then these gallant drivers swung their six Napoleon guns into action, the left wheels in the air, their right wheels plowing furrow in*

> *the ground as they made the turn. Then came the ringing commands, 'With canister, load!' 'Commence firing!' and the battle was on.*

In the next twenty minutes, forty-four of the sixty cannoneers were killed or wounded.

General John Gibbon, who, seeing nearly all the men of the left gun of the battery being killed or wounded and the battery in danger of being captured, [Hogart continued], in the full uniform of his rank assisted his detached volunteers in working one of the guns, thus aiding in repulsing the enemy.

This was the Battle of Antietam outside Sharpsburg, Maryland. On that day, September 17, 1862, more Americans died than on any other day, including D-Day and September 11, 2001.

One of the amazing things about this horrific battle is that

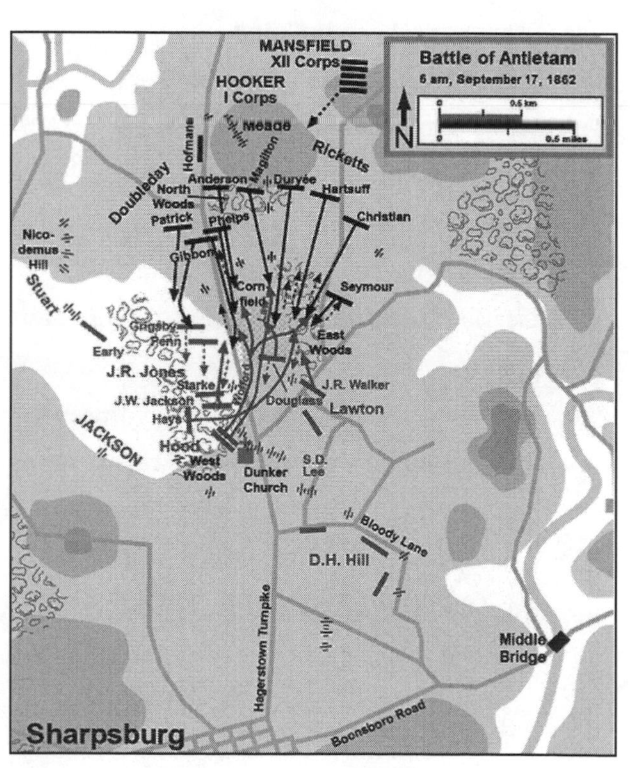

BATTLE OF ANTIETAM

the Iron Brigade continued to function as an effective unit. In the brief account above, significant events happen in the course of just a few minutes. We see a major assume command of a regiment, then the responsibilities of a colonel, with no time for transition, and we see a general take on the role of several cannoneers, normally enlisted soldiers, who would typically have been assigned to load, aim, and fire a cannon. The cannons kept firing and the enemy's assault was stalled—all because individuals filled in when and where needed to keep the whole brigade functioning.

The Brigade had been formed a little over a year before Antietam. The farm boys from Indiana and Wisconsin who comprised the regiment shared a common bond: they were from much farther west than most of the soldiers fighting in Virginia and Maryland. Most of their first year was engaged in training and building, much of it outside Washington, D.C., in Northern Virginia. They built Fort Craig, which is near the site where the Pentagon stands today, part of a string of forts in the Virginia cities of Arlington and Alexandria built to defend Washington from attack. The Brigade's men were among the troops who found the "Quaker guns" (logs painted black to deceive the enemy at a distance) defending Upton Hill near Falls Church and abandoned fortifications around Manassas. (Both of these episodes proved embarrassing for General George McClellan, who always overestimated the strength of the enemy.)

The biggest turning point for the Brigade came when John Gibbon became its commander. A West Point graduate and career army officer, Gibbon was also a remarkable leader who made the Brigade one of the most successful fighting units during the Civil War. Ironically, being put in command of an infantry brigade of volunteers was not Gibbon's ideal assignment. As a regular army officer, he had a low opinion of volunteer units. But he took on the challenge of instilling discipline and pride in his group.

He pulled out his books on drills for infantry, and began drilling his soldiers like few other commanders. He also required all of his officers to wake early and join in the drills—which earned him respect from the average soldier.

Gibbon even went beyond the standard uniform and ordered distinctive black felt Hardee hats for the soldiers, hats that were normally reserved for dress uniforms. He also outfitted his entire brigade with white leggings. The fancy hats and white leggings, along with the precision marching and maneuvering, earned them the name "Black Hat Brigade" before they became known as the Iron Brigade. The raiment made this group of volunteers from the farms of Indiana and Wisconsin look like an elite force, as the Hardee hats were much more popular with officers than enlisted soldiers. And an elite force is what they became.

Soldiers of the Iron Brigade

The white leggings proved impractical when they started marching great distances and fighting as front line troops, but the black Hardee hats remained the group's signature. This is not unlike the idea of using a unique uniform to build a special identity and esprit de corps, as do the Army Rangers and the Green Berets.

In addition to creating special uniforms for his force, Gibbon also insisted that his soldiers wear the uniforms correctly. Once, early in his command, when he saw one of his soldiers on guard duty wearing his uniform correctly, he relieved him of his duty, marched him past the others who were disheveled and gave that soldier a 24-hour pass, to show the others what was expected.

A year of this intensive training and working together building forts and other tasks created a remarkable force. In his memoirs *Personal Recollections of the Civil War*, Gibbon wrote:

> *School teaching of any kind is at best a laborious business but when the scholars number several thousand and the head teacher has to assist him but few who know even the A.B.C. of the subject to be taught, the task becomes Herculean. In this case, however, the quick intelligence of the scholars (the volunteers) smoothed over many of the rough places and served to nullify even the strong opposition exhibited to a regular officer being in command. Regular drills were instituted and where the regimental commander knew nothing of the drill, I sometimes took command myself, and then it was wonderful to see the transformation; how eagerly my explanations were listened to by both officers and men, and how intelligently the commands were executed.*

When the Western volunteers in black hats finally saw combat, it was intense. They had four major battles in three weeks in the summer of 1862 and sustained casualties of more than 75% during that period. In most of these battles they were directly facing off against some of the

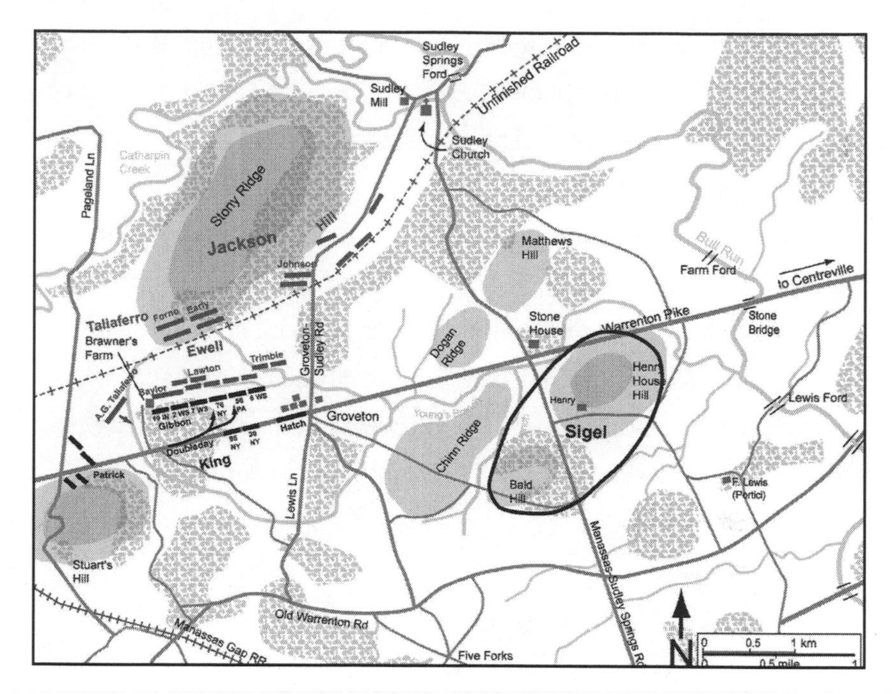

BATTLE OF BRAWNER'S FARM

Confederate army's best troops.

In their very first combat experience, for example, they stumbled upon the famous Stonewall Brigade at Brawner's farm near Manassas the day before the Second Battle of Bull Run (Manassas). Both sides lined up just fifty yards from each other and fought for more than two hours. It was a remarkable standoff in that neither side gained or lost a foot of ground.

It is often said that there is no substitute for experience, but the Battle of Brawner's Farm proved that enough high quality training can indeed match experience.

The unit had only four days in their base camp at Upton Hill, near Falls Church, to rest between battles after Brawner's Farm and the Second Battle of Bull Run (Manassas). The rest must have been very welcome. This high-ground fort on the border between Arlington County and Falls Church was familiar and deep enough into the Union defenses around

Washington to offer a real break. Nearly a year earlier Julia Ward Howe had visited Upton Hill with some other well-known abolitionists and been so impressed with the fort and troops that she was inspired to write "The Battle Hymn of the Republic."

As reported in Indiana at Antietam: Report of the Indiana Antietam Monument Commission (1911), this Black Hat Brigade earned the name Iron Brigade in the Battle of South Mountain, a few days before Antietam, and just two weeks after they had fought with distinction at Brawner's Farm and the Second Battle of Bull Run (Manassas). John Callis, a Union officer from Wisconsin, heard the story directly from General George McClellan:

> *It was during the Battle of South Mountain, my headquarters were where I could see every move of the troops on the pike with my glass. I saw the men fighting against great odds. When General Hooker came in great haste for orders, I asked him what men were fighting on the pike. He replied: General Gibbon's Brigade of Western men. I said: They must be made of iron. Hooker replied: By the Eternal, they are iron! If you had seen them at Bull Run as I did, you would know them to be iron.*

Leadership Insights

In the classic *The Art of War*, Sun Tzu provides insights into commanders and training that reflect some secrets of the Iron Brigade's success: The commander must be a military professional. This requires confidence and detachment. You must maintain dignity and order. You must control what your men see and hear. They must follow you without knowing your plans. You can reinvent your men's roles.

JOHN GIBBON

Clearly, General Gibbon was such a professional. He inspired dignity and brought order to a group that did not have it and, as a result of his actions, he was able to reinvent the roles of his soldiers when he needed to. Or, to be more accurate, they were able to reinvent their own roles when they saw the need.

On training, which was a central element of what Gibbon brought to the Iron Brigade, Sun Tzu said,

> *You must control your soldiers with esprit de corps. You must bring them together by winning victories. You must get them to believe in you. Make it easy for people to know what to do by training your people. Your people will then obey you. If you do not make it easy for people to know what to do, you won't train your people. They then will not obey. Make your commands easy to follow. You must understand the way a crowd thinks.*

Gibbon's upgrades in the soldiers' uniforms helped create esprit de corps, as did his consistent training and his insistence that his directions be followed by enlisted men as well as officers. When the need arose, the men knew how to perform.

Regarding the analytical skills a commander must have, Sun Tzu said,

> *You must ask: Which government has the right philosophy? Which commander has the skill? Which method of command works? Which group of forces has the strength? Which officers and men have the training? Which rewards and punishments make sense? This tells when you will win and when you will lose. Some commanders perform this analysis. If you use these commanders, you will win. Keep them.*

John Gibbon was known for doing exactly that: considering all angles of a situation and applying good judgment. In 1869, for example, General Francis Walker addressed these traits in Gibbon in a paper called "General Gibbon in the Second Corps," published in *Personal Recollections of the War of the Rebellion*. Walker wrote,

> *General Gibbon's characteristics were, from the first, fully manifest. Intelligence is perhaps the single word which best describes him as a commander of troops, whether in the field, on the march, or in battle. There was nothing dull, or heavy, or commonplace*

> *about his performance of any duty. He looked fully at every situation; saw it for himself; saw it clearly; studied it in the light of experience and of military knowledge; and as the result made up his opinion and took his course of action. His powers of perception and his powers of reflection were well balanced; and both faculties were actively used whenever he had any military duty to perform. He knew just what he was going to do and just why he was going to do it, whereas many of us have known more than one general officer, not at all incapable, who saw just far enough ahead and around to get his brigade or division or corps into action, without any clear conception of what he was really trying to do.*

As we see from the excerpts above, a winning leader needs a keen intellect and the discipline to look at all the elements of a situation to plot a course of action that will lead to the ultimate goal. But there is more to Gibbon than this ancient wisdom of being the right commander and using training effectively. Let's explore what Gibbon did to help make the Iron Brigade such a unique force.

Attrition happens in every organization. Individuals with certain skills and knowledge leave, and that gap must be filled in some way to keep the group performing well. For most organizations this attrition happens over time, and whereas it is always a challenge, one hopes that there are not too many open positions at once. At Antietam, the Iron Brigade was losing hundreds of soldiers and officers within minutes and yet essential roles were filled and performed quickly. This is an extreme example, but a useful one.

The field of organizational psychology maintains that high-performance human resource systems that use high levels of personnel selection, training, mentoring, performance appraisal, rewards, cross-functional teams, and knowledge sharing among employees increases the performance of the organization in important ways.

This theory is evident in the story of the Iron Brigade. Gibbon insisted on high performance from his troops. He expected them to be the equals of the best regular army troops, and they were. He rewarded those who complied (for example, the 24-hour pass to the guard who was in full uniform). Gibbon was also demanding of his officers and, through a combination of recruitment, promotion and discipline, he was able to build the leadership team that helped him carry out his reforms and training.

The article "A Relational Model of How High-Performance Work Systems Work" by Gittell, Seidner and Wimbush in the March-April 2010 issue of Organizational Science explored the role of high-performance human resource systems in a study of nine urban hospitals. They looked at how groups of employees with different roles/skills interacted and performed in an environment that included a high degree of training, cross-functional teams, and accountability for performance.

A key finding: these practices build ties between different roles in the organization, so that people in different functions understand what the others are doing better. This greatly enhances communications and allows for seamless operations and greater efficiency.

Unlike relationships that are based on personal ties, the relationships found

> *in relational coordination are based instead on ties between roles. [These] work practices ... are expected to foster relationships of shared goals, shared knowledge, and mutual respect among employees whose work is interdependent, with or without the presence of personal ties. This feature allows for the interchangeability of employees, allowing employees to come and go without missing a beat, an important consideration for organizations that strive to achieve high levels of performance... Role-based relationships may require greater organizational investments to foster than personal ties—for example, designing cross-functional boundary-spanning roles and cross-functional performance measurement systems versus hosting after-work parties – but they are also more robust to staffing changes that occur.*
>
> *- (Gittell, Seidner, and Wimbush, 2010)*

During the Civil War, there was no lack of personal connection between the soldiers. In most cases, they all came from the same town, where their families had known each other for generations. I am sure one of Gibbon's challenges was to take these volunteers with strong personal connections and make them into a highly trained organization where everyone knows not only his own role but also the roles of all of those around them. The Iron Brigade was able to function so well in such extreme circumstances only because of the extensive training, high standards of performance, mentoring, and other high-performance human resource systems Gibbon employed. Perhaps the training was so good because Gibbon was an artillery officer and needed to pull out his infantry training books to figure out what his footsoldiers should know and be able to do. Gibbon did not assume he knew the material. Instead he made sure he was teaching all the skills "by the book." The troops also soon understood they were being taught the right way to do things and they worked to meet Gibbon's expectations. In the Battle of Brawner's Farm, for example, the brigade lined up in arrow-traight lines as if they were on parade. Such precision and focus on details may not have helped them in this battle, but it demonstrates the effectiveness of their training and that they would be in perfect formation, even under heavy fire in their first combat experience.

While most modern business, government, or nonprofit sectors will never see anything remotely like the living hell the Iron Brigade experienced, leaders today can learn to implement the high standards, extensive training, and other systems that will assure that their organization can tackle any obstacle known or unknown that might come along.

CHAPTER 11

The Importance of Innovation: John Mosby

On December 6, 1864, with the end of the war just six months away, the South was losing the war on most fronts. Lee and Grant were engaged in trench war outside Richmond, the two great generals headquartered less than one mile apart.

That evening, while many in the Confederate army were malnourished and in rags, an officer in a new uniform, complete with new polished knee-high cavalry boots, a hat with an ostrich feather, and a cape lined in red, came to have dinner with General Lee. John Mosby had been a scout for J.E.B. Stuart. During that time, he had been very impressed with the great style that Stuart always had. Now, several years later, he was dressing the part of a dapper cavalry officer in good times. As he rode up on a healthy fast steed and walked about, he must have stood out as some strange vision amid all the other soldiers in rags.

The red cape was steeped in symbolism. Julius Caesar wore a famous red cape in battle so his soldiers could see that he was with them, and as a sign of bravery. Mosby's early commander and model J.E.B. Stuart wore the red cape, which Mosby then adopted, as did General George Patton (who as a boy knew Mosby in his later years) in battle during World War II. Mosby was a student of the classics and understood the power of evoking symbols of the great leaders of the past.

Unlike many other Civil War generals, Mosby had had no military training prior to the war, nor had he gone to West Point or the Virginia Military Institute. He was an attorney who had studied classical literature before studying law. Everything he learned about the military he picked up in "on the job training."

The first two years of the war he served as a capable, but low-level, cavalry scout. J.E.B. Stuart saw the Mosby's talent, however, and allowed him to recruit a command to serve in Northern Virginia and keep pressure on the Washington defenses.

The Mosby experiment was a great success. One victory followed another. In one of his early actions, Mosby led a midnight raid on the Fairfax Courthouse, many miles behind Union lines, with just twenty-eight soldiers.

He captured a Union brigadier general and sixty horses and escaped without a shot being fired. Mosby did not win every engagement, but his track record was astonishing. Largely due to this record he continued to recruit more troops to his command. The night Mosby sat down to eat with Lee, Mosby commanded 800 of the best-armed and best-supplied troops in the Confederate forces, troops who were among the most successful in battle.

The purpose for his visit was to get permission to grow his command from one battalion to two, to expand his range of operations. He'd put the request on paper, writing it on General Lee's desk during his visit:

Hon. James A. Seddon, Secretary of War:
SIR: I beg leave to recommend, in order to

> *secure greater efficiency in my command, that it be divided into two battalions, each to be commanded by a major. The scope of duties devolving upon me being of a much wider extent than on officers of the same rank in regular service...*

Lee blessed the plan, and Mosby was promoted to a full colonel. Notice what Mosby did here: In this statement, he acknowledged that his responsibilities had graduated to the level of a general, even though he was "just" a colonel. The interesting story, of course, is not that Mosby was successful, but rather, why he was so successful.

So here's the key question: What made Mosby so effective that he was able to transition from a private with no military training to one of the most effective commanders of the Confederate army with a rank of full colonel and duties on par with a brigadier general?

The keys to his success were many, but at their core was innovation. Because Mosby was not trained at a military college, he was not steeped in the tactics and strategies of the Napoleonic wars, as were the other military leaders of the day. He was instead free to think practically about the current circumstances and the tools at his disposal and create a new model of how to fight effectively. Let us look at some of the elements that made Mosby's command hard to beat.

Partisan rangers

In 1862, the Confederate Congress passed the Partisan Ranger Act. This law allowed authorized officers to recruit and equip quasi-independent forces. One of the key elements attracting Mosby was that this act authorized these rangers to keep and distribute captured goods that were not deemed to be of direct military value. Weapons and horses that were captured in action were sent to the Confederate army, but other goods, including food, clothes, money, or other valuables, were distributed among the rangers. These goods were in addition to their standard salary from the Confederate government. Mosby understood that with this authorization he would have a great advantage in recruiting soldiers and motivating them.

Military leaders had a very dim view of rangers, and for good reason. Many ranger groups were little more that bands of robbers, like Quantril's Rangers in Missouri, which after the war became the Jesse James Gang. By 1863, when Mosby was given his own command, the regular army had integrated most of the ranger groups that had been established, and they were under normal military command. General J.E.B. Stuart encouraged Mosby to set up his command as a regular cavalry group because he had such a low opinion of rangers, but Mosby was persistent that being authorized under the Partisan Ranger Act would be an advantage. And Mosby was able to avoid the pitfalls that some ranger groups fell into, such as devolving into a gang of robbers, by keeping his command focused on military targets and setting the example of not taking his share of the riches after many of the actions. This approach called for high principles, but Mosby had a lifelong history of fighting against corruption, and he was able to use the best of the Partisan Ranger Act and avoid the worst.

Base of operation

Because Mosby was operating outside Washington, D.C., on the edge of one of the largest concentrations of federal forces, he knew that if he established a base camp, his group would be an easy target. So he chose not to establish one. Instead, after each battle action, his soldiers spread out and slept in barns and farmhouses throughout the countryside.

When Union forces went on a raid to round up Mosby's Rangers, they were lucky to capture a few of them.

CAVALRY FIGHT AT MOUNT ZION.

When the time came for action, Mosby passed the word to meet at a certain time and place, which frequently changed. His forces did not know their mission until they had assembled and were on their way. This also eliminated the chance of the Union learning where he was going to strike in advance. No other military group in the Civil War operated quite like this, and it was a source of constant frustration to the Union forces. The fact that his group was hard to find, in addition to Mosby himself being frequently injured but always returning, added to his reputation as the "Gray Ghost."

Weapons and training

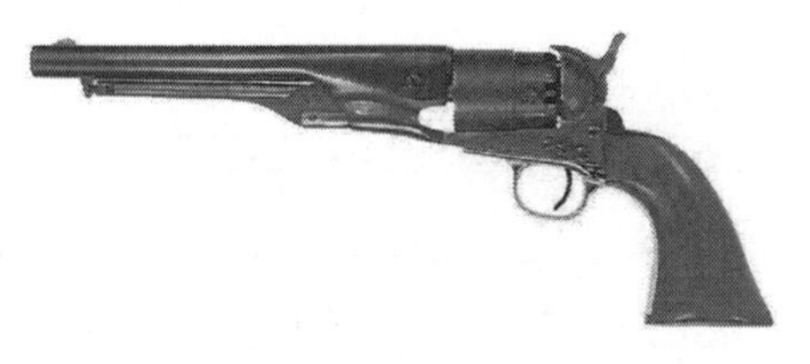

1860 ARMY COLT REVOLVER

As mentioned before, the military leaders on both sides during the Civil War were steeped in tactics that came from Napoleonic Wars. At that time, the key tactic was to maneuver large groups of soldiers into lines for attack. The eighteenth- and nineteenth-century flintlock muskets used by the infantry were too inaccurate and even unreliable to worry about target practice. Instead, the idea was to line up enough soldiers so that even if a large percentage of muskets did not fire, there would be an adequate volley of lead balls going down the field. While the cavalry handled operations somewhat differently, they still focused on maneuvering large groups into lines for combat. And the legacy of inaccurate firearms still made the sword the dominant weapon in training.

Cavalry soldiers, both Union and Confederate, were outfitted with a sword on their left hip to be drawn by the right hand (making it the principal weapon), a pistol to be drawn by the left hand, and a short rifle called a carbine. In previous wars (with the exception of the short Mexican War just before the Civil War), the firearms had been single-shot weapons. As a result, cavalry training had not caught up to the potential of the new six-shooter pistols that they were carrying.

Mosby understood that the sword was completely ineffective against guns. He understood that the carbine was a two-handed weapon and could not be fired effectively while riding a horse. He also fully grasped the potential of a relatively new invention, the six-shooter revolver invented by Samuel Colt in 1839, who was inspired by the ratcheting mechanism used to raise the anchor on ships. While a first-generation revolver was issued to cavalry and officers in the Mexican War of the 1850s, the new second-generation 1860 Army Colt Revolver (and Navy Revolver) came out just before the Civil War. They were reliable and effective weapons with great firepower at close range. Mosby understood that this weapon could be used as a force multiplier, particularly since his soldiers were highly proficient in its use. In 1906, John W. Munson wrote this about the training of Mosby's command in his book *Reminiscences of a Mosby*

Guerrilla:

> *Contrary to a popular impression we did not carry carbines at any time during the war. Each of Mosby's men was armed with two muzzle-loading Colt's army revolvers of forty-four caliber. They were worn in belt holsters. Some few who could afford it, or who had succeeded in capturing extra pistols or who wanted to gratify a sort of vanity, wore an extra pair in their saddle-holsters or stuck into their boot leg. These weapons were extremely deadly and effective in the hand-to-hand engagements in which our men indulged. Long and frequent practice had made every man in the Command a good shot... It was no uncommon thing for one of our men to gallop by a tree at full tilt, and put three bullets into its trunk in succession. This sort of shooting left the enemy with a good many empty saddles after an engagement... ... The Federal cavalry generally fought with sabers... and Mosby used to say they were as useless against a skillfully handled revolver as the wooden swords of harlequins.*

Leadership Insights

Many of the greatest leaders in the world have been innovators. By creating a competitive environment with a new set of rules that they have mastered, they can lead in a dominant way until the competition catches up.

Innovation comes in many forms, from minor changes in process to significant shifts in paradigms. One of the most compelling innovation theories is that described in Blue Ocean Strategy by W. Chan Kim and Renée Mauborgne. When you are competing in a market full of similar offers, the ocean is red with the blood of competition. When significant innovation takes place, your product or service is so different that the competition becomes irrelevant, and you have found a market space that is blue ocean: you are the only one in this area of the market. Eventually, competitors will learn the new game, but if the innovative leap is large enough it might be some time before the others can truly catch up.

JOHN MOSBY

One of the key steps to blue ocean innovation is to break from the mindset that you should measure performance based on your company or industry. For Mosby, his company was Confederate Cavalry and his industry was mid-nineteenth-century military. If he had built his organization around the best practices of these models, he might have created a very good cavalry unit, but he would not have had anywhere near the success that he did. The industry model would have had a base camp that would have been overrun, and it would have used the standard set of cavalry weapons and training. It is very likely that if he had been educated in the military standards of the time it would have been much more difficult for him to have innovated.

Central to Mauborgne and Kim's work is the idea of "value innovation." In the examples of significant innovation that they studied, the cost of the product went down at the same time the value went up!

Applying this idea to Mosby's leadership, we can see that Mosby was able to significantly reduce the cost of his command to the Confederate Army by largely self-funding the operation. In order to volunteer for his group, a soldier needed to supply his own horse and weapons. By capturing large supplies of equipment from the Union army, his group was always well equipped with the best materials his competitors could offer. Through the Partisan Ranger Act, he could legally compensate his soldiers with contraband, long after his government no longer had the means to pay and supply the rest of the military. This all made it very easy for Lee to agree to allow Mosby to expand his command.

What is known as "buyer value" in today's market terms was known as "effectiveness" in the context of the Civil War. Mosby's primary strategic mission was not to win big battles but to tie up disproportional Union resources, preventing them from being sent to the front. By creating a constant sense of risk around Washington with his hit-and-run actions, the Union felt a need to keep tens of thousands of soldiers and related supplies all around for protection. In Virginia, the 30-mile radius around the city of Washington was a huge armed camp, and most of it was because of the elusive and highly effective Mosby's Rangers.

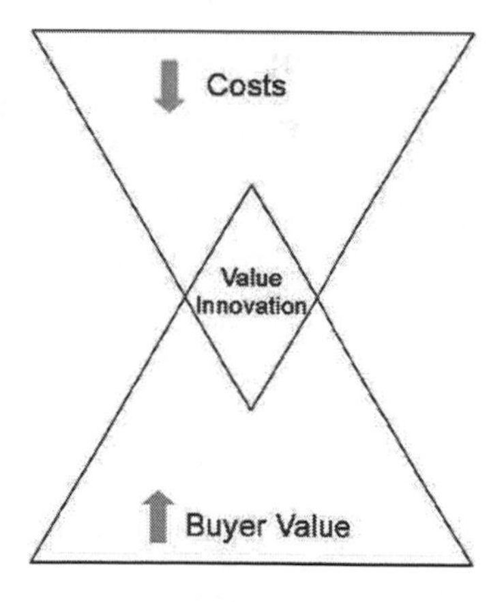

Using speed and firepower to overcome larger opponents, living off the land, having no need for bases or supply lines, and offering monetary incentive for success were all radical departures from military doctrine—they were true blue ocean innovations.

Though managing people effectively and obtaining incremental efficiencies are all good and can be the building block for success in any organization, there is no substitute for innovation. Good companies are managed well, and great ones use innovation to create new markets and ultimately revolutionize their industries.

CHAPTER 12

Be Your Best Leader

How do you take all of these historical examples, research, and theo ries about leadership and apply them? While there are common lessons that can be applied to any leader, the formula for each individual will be different. Here are my recommendations.

Build on Your Best

First and foremost, be true to yourself. Know your own strengths and build a leadership style that takes full advantage of these strengths.

It follows, then, that you would be well advised to do some self-analysis. Numerous tools exist to help you uncover your natural strengths. One is Strengthfinder, an online survey tool from Gallup. Another is the Herrmann Whole Brain Model, which is a great tool for understanding how you process information, and how others may think differently from you. Other good tools also exist, such as the Meyers-Briggs survey, which can be wonderfully helpful in understanding who you are and what are your strengths.

To achieve your best potential, you must build on your best elements.

You are not going to be a charismatic Phil Sheridan if you are shy and introverted, and you are not going to be the macro-strategist if your strength is paying attention to details. To be great, use your natural skills to their best advantage.

Overcome Negative Patterns

Research from the Gallup Organization has shown that the greatest results can be achieved by focusing on skills and developing them. If you have a reactive pattern that is adversely affecting your decision making, like Custer's pattern of reckless charging, you need to address it. Just as understanding your strengths is important, if your trigger-response patterns are getting in your way, you need to reprogram those patterns so they do not limit your full potential. This requires a high degree of honest self-assessment.

Move Forward

If you are going to be a leader, then set goals and achieve them. It is not enough to have a title like manager, director, president, vice-president, commander, etc. To be a leader, you must act in the best way to move your group forward, to make progress.

Momentum is one of the most powerful leadership dynamics. Success begets success, so set goals that you believe can be achieved. This will enhance the position of your group and create a positive momentum that can be the foundation for greater success. Momentum is the most powerful motivator: in a study of worker motivation, progress was more important than salary, benefits, working conditions, or anything else.

An essential element of creating momentum is to have a common and well-articulated goal, so when your group sees that change is happening, it is clear that they are moving forward. Action without a clear and well-understood goal may not create the all-important momentum that you need.

Having a clear mission is the first step in having a strategic plan for achieving goals two to five years out. Shorter-term plans tend to be operational plans with more details, and plans that look out ten to twenty years tend to be vision exercises that focus on what could be someday. Both short-term plans and long-term visioning can be very useful, but they are not strategic plans. The purpose of a strategic plan is to set goals and key steps or indicators that will demonstrate that the organization is moving towards those goals. This becomes the crucial link between actions and goals.

During the Civil War, strategic planning did not have the role it plays in most modern organizations. The South's basic plan was to try to win, from European powers, recognition of their status as an independent nation.

The North's goal was to force the South to surrender, and the ideas about how to achieve this goal changed over time. One could make the case that both sides would have been better served with a more overt strategic planning approach to their goals.

Inherent with movement is risk. In comparing Mosby and Custer, we saw the difference between thoughtful, strategic risk taking and knee-jerk, irrational risk taking. Risk has a bad reputation because of its potential negative consequences, but without thoughtful risk there can be no forward movement.

What is true for investment is also true for leadership. Avoiding all risk is a recipe for stagnation. The better course is to seek a balance of well-considered risk with the possibility for great strategic gain.

Develop Organizational Capacity

Great leaders build great organizations. Structurally, you can use the tools of high-performance human resource systems, tools such as training cross-functional teams that can build cohesion and understanding of what different groups within the organization do. This cross-functional pollination promotes new and productive communication patterns within the organizations that reach across silos within the organizational structure. Good performance evaluations and fair systems of reward and punishment can build morale, as people realize they are in a merit-based organization.

Build balanced teams wherever possible. While individuals do not need to be good at everything, the most effective teams will have a mix of strengths that cover all the bases. If your strength is implementing, for example, team up with a good intelligence gatherer and a strategic thinker. Teams are great places to experiment with cross-functional groups. When you find that combination of team members with the right mix of skills and personalities to take on big issues, use that team again. When the right mix is in place, the power of a great team can be much more than the sum of the parts.

Demonstrating your willingness to change direction based on new information and perhaps take a non-traditional course of action (the definition of a decisive leader) can affect the entire organization in positive ways. Once people see that new information is being used, the whole organization will gather, transmit, and process information better. Conversely, when leadership is stuck in the status quo, the organization shuts down its information-gathering activities, and the organization is much more likely to be adversely affected by an external force they were ignoring.

Finally, given that most organizations having a governance board of some kind, it is important for all parties to understand their roles. A well-focused governance board can be an important check and balance on the organization's finances, but also the champions of the mission and co-creators of the strategic plan.

Innovate

Benchmarking is a great strategy if your goal is to be slightly above average. If you seek to set a new standard in your field, you cannot get there by just looking within that field, which is what benchmarking essentially does. You need to look to other fields and innovate. Using the tools of Blue Ocean Strategy, look at where you can make a value innovation that offers higher performance at a lower cost.

The beauty of innovation is that any organization can do it. It does not matter if you are large or small; you can change your field by setting aside conventional wisdom and thinking about the value your organization delivers, the potential needs of your customers, and the strengths of your group. If you can create a blue ocean market, you will make all competition largely irrelevant. Large-scale Proctor & Gamble spends 50% more than its closest competitor on research and development of new products. Innovation is central to its corporate identity and the key reason the company has had such enduring success. Small-scale (at the time) Steve Jobs and Steve Wozniak founded Apple Computers in Steve Jobs' parents' garage. Jobs and Wozniak did not look to the IBM mainframe model that was the computer industry model at the time but looked to fill a need most people did not even know they had—personal computing. Apple has focused on innovation ever since, and in the process influenced personal computers, laptops, smart phones, and more.

Focus on Opportunity

Sun Tzu said, "You can recognize the opportunity for victory; you don't create it." We do not control all the forces around us, but if we are taking the right steps, and are open to and looking for opportunity, that we will find it.

The power of focus is amazing, and the strengths-based paradigm is the key to understanding where to put your focus for greatest growth and development. As a leader, you must be both open to finding new opportunities and actively scanning for these opportunities. Years ago, I read in a skiing magazine about how one can ski through the most treacherous environment in a relatively effortless way. The key was to focus all your attention on the good path. It did not matter if there was a sheer cliff on one side and a large boulder or tree on the other side—if there was a nice snowy spot a few feet wide, you were in great shape so long as you put all you attention on the good spot.

Your focus determines exactly where you will go. You do not need to worry too much how to get there, so long as you maintain your focus on the place you want to be.

While the skiing analogy is a long way from the Civil War, it demonstrates the power of focus on opportunity. You can see the same dynamic at play with Grant at Vicksburg or Lee at Chancellorsville. Both generals were in a hazardous environment with many more chances to fail than to succeed. But both generals were able to see the opportunity that exists in almost any situation and put their full focus on that narrow path. In the process they grabbed victory from the jaws of defeat.

This speaks to the power of optimism. Those who focus on the good spot will go there, and those who focus on the rocks will hit them. This requires us to have a good vision and strategic plan, so we know where we are trying to go. As Sun Tzu advised, it means recognizing the opportunities to achieve your goals as they present themselves and acting on them. And if you are looking for the opportunities, they will appear.

APPENDIX A

Leadership Lessons

Through the examples of these Civil War stories, we have explored numerous theories and studies related to leadership. Remember the microscope metaphor: that as you adjust the focal point in and out, different levels of the subject come into and out of focus. Each leadership lesson has a different focal point. Though the lessons are drawn from many academic disciplines, when taken together, each lesson helps build a fuller picture of the leader's role. Here we briefly recap each of those lessons.

Chapter 1: Mosby: The Power of Momentum

• Momentum is one of the most important concepts in achieving goals. Build a track record of smaller successes that will help achieve larger ones.

• Successful leaders study and learn from great leaders of the past.

• Leaders who project confidence in nonverbal ways are 87% more likely to succeed.

• In a competitive environment, change your mode of operation to keep your opponents guessing and increase your chances of success.

• Know how an opponent will see and process your actions is key to gaining the upper hand. Being able to think several steps ahead, then putting yourself in the mind of others, is key to knowing the right actions to take.

• People want leaders to address their needs for trust, compassion, stability, and hope.

For further reading:

• Buckingham, M. (2001). *Now, Discover Your Strengths.* New York: The Free Press.

• Pentland, A. (2010, January-February). Defend your research: We can measure the power of charisma. *Harvard Business Review.*

• Rath, T. & Conchie, B. (2008). *Strengths-Based Leadership.* New York: Gallup Press.

Chapter 2: Custer: Understanding Your Own Reactions

• Our reactive patterns of behavior can get in the way of good decision making.

• Irrational decisions made during periods of stress can create cognitive patterns that will cause the person to repeat similar irrational decisions.

• With intention, you can replace old cognitive patterns with positive alternative reactions using a process called cognitive-behavioral therapy.

For further reading:

Andrade, E.B. & Ariely, D. (2009, May). Organizational behavior and human decision processes. *Elsevier Journal 109(1).*

Chapter 3: McClellan: The Perfectionist's Dilemma

• To understand your strengths and weaknesses, understand the roles of each of the four quadrants of the brain and their related cognitive patterns.

• To achieve greatness, do not focus on balance or weaknesses, but rather on developing strengths to their full potential.

Chapter 4: Grant and Lee, Chancellorsville and Vicksburg

• Greatness comes from focusing on strengths.

• The best teams are made up of people with complementary strengths. The two great leadership teams of the Civil War vet this persective:

o Confederate: Robert E. Lee (strategic thinker); J.E.B. Stuart (intelligence gatherer); Stonewall Jackson (determined implementer)

o Union: Ulysses S. Grant (strategic thinker); Phil Sheridan (intelligence gatherer); William Sherman (determined implementer).

• Success often lies in recognizing and taking advantage of opportunity when it arises. Don't planning to the point that you cannot see and act on opportunities.

Chapter 5: Lincoln: A Compelling Mission

• A clear and compelling mission is essential for motivating a group to achieve great things. The greater the sacrifice that is asked, the more noble the mission must be.

• Missions with real focus come at some political cost.

Chapter 6: Stonewall Jackson

• Progress is more important to motivation than compensation, benefits, or working conditions. Feeling that you are making a difference is the single most motivating factor.

For further reading:

Amabile, T.M. & Kramer, S.J. (2010, January-February). What really motivates workers. *Harvard Business Review 88(1)*, pp. 44–45.

Chapter 7: Charles Stone: Professionalism and the Mandate of Governance and Management

• How one handles oneself in adversity can have a great impact on personal reputations.

• Those in both Governance and Management roles should understand the unique role they both pay in organizational success.

• Corporate boards are responsible for greater financial oversight, thanks to the Sarbanes Oxley legislation,

• Good use of a governance board can help any organization not only have good financial oversight, but a good mission and strategic direction.

For further reading:

Gottlieb, H. Creating the Future. http://hildygottlieb.com/

Chapter 8: J.E.B. Stuart: Decisive Leadership

• Understanding the strengths of your group can be central to your success.

• Decisive leadership is the ability to change direction based on new information, and to take unconventional directions if circumstances dictate it is the best course.

• Focusing energy on the narrow path of opportunity has great power.

• The leader's demeanor influences the energy and behavior of the group. Negative or fearful reactions are amplified in followers. Leaders do well to act calmly in times of stress.

• Escape and victory rely on the element of surprise, which is an infinite resource.

• Success builds confidence and momentum, which in turn leads to more success.

For further reading:

Ishida, J. (2008). Decisiveness (OSIPP Discussion Paper 08E002). Osaka University School of International Public Policy. Available from http://econpapers.repec.org/paper/ospwpaper/08e002.htm

Chapter 9: Phil Sheridan: The Power of Personality

• Charisma encompasses nonverbal communication signals such as tone, gesture, expression, and face-to-face interaction.

• Understanding different levels of nonverbal communication can help leaders better interact with others.

For further reading:

Pentland, A. (2008). *Honest Signals.* Cambridge, MA: MIT Press.

Chapter 10: John Gibbon: The Role of Training

• Commanders should have the following traits: professionalism, confidence, detachment, dignity, a sense of order, the ability to build esprit de corps, ability to train, ability to assess strengths, understanding of how to effectively reward and punish.

• High-performance human resource systems are H.R. and management practices that include good recruitment/selection practices, training, mentoring, performance appraisals, reward systems, use of cross-functional teams, and knowledge sharing.

For further reading:

Gittell, J.H., Seidner, R., & Wimbush, J. (2010, March-April). A relational model of how high-performance work systems work. Organizational Science 21(2), pp. 490–506.

Chapter 11: Mosby: The Importance of Innovation

• While there are many avenues to success, perhaps the greatest success comes from innovation.

• To be successful at innovation, set aside the notion of benchmarking, because it only leads to incremental improvement and obscures the insight that will change your field.

• Central to Blue Ocean Strategy is changing the market to such an extent that the competition is irrelevant.

• Value innovation is the act of both reducing the cost of your product or service and at the same time increasing the perceived value of the product or service.

For further reading:

Kim, C. & Mauborgne, R. (2005). *Blue Ocean Strategy.* Boston MA: Harvard Business School Press.

Appendix B

Parks and Places

The places where these historic examples of leadership happened are also a part of the leadership story. Though the individuals of that time are long gone, many of the historic sites have been preserved and interpreted so visitors today can see for themselves the places that helped shape America.

While the primary goal of this book is to examine and study leadership, a secondary goal is to encourage an interest in American history. If you have been engaged by the stories featured in this book and would like to expand your knowledge of these events further, a great next step is to visit the featured sites. Many of these sites are in the Northern Virginia region. Even more of the sites fall within an area known as "The Journey through Hallowed Ground." This larger region stretches from Gettysburg, PA, to Charlottesville, VA, and includes more site associated with the founding and early development of America than any other region in the country.

Below is an alphabetical list of the historic sites mentioned in this book and some information on who owns and manages these properties

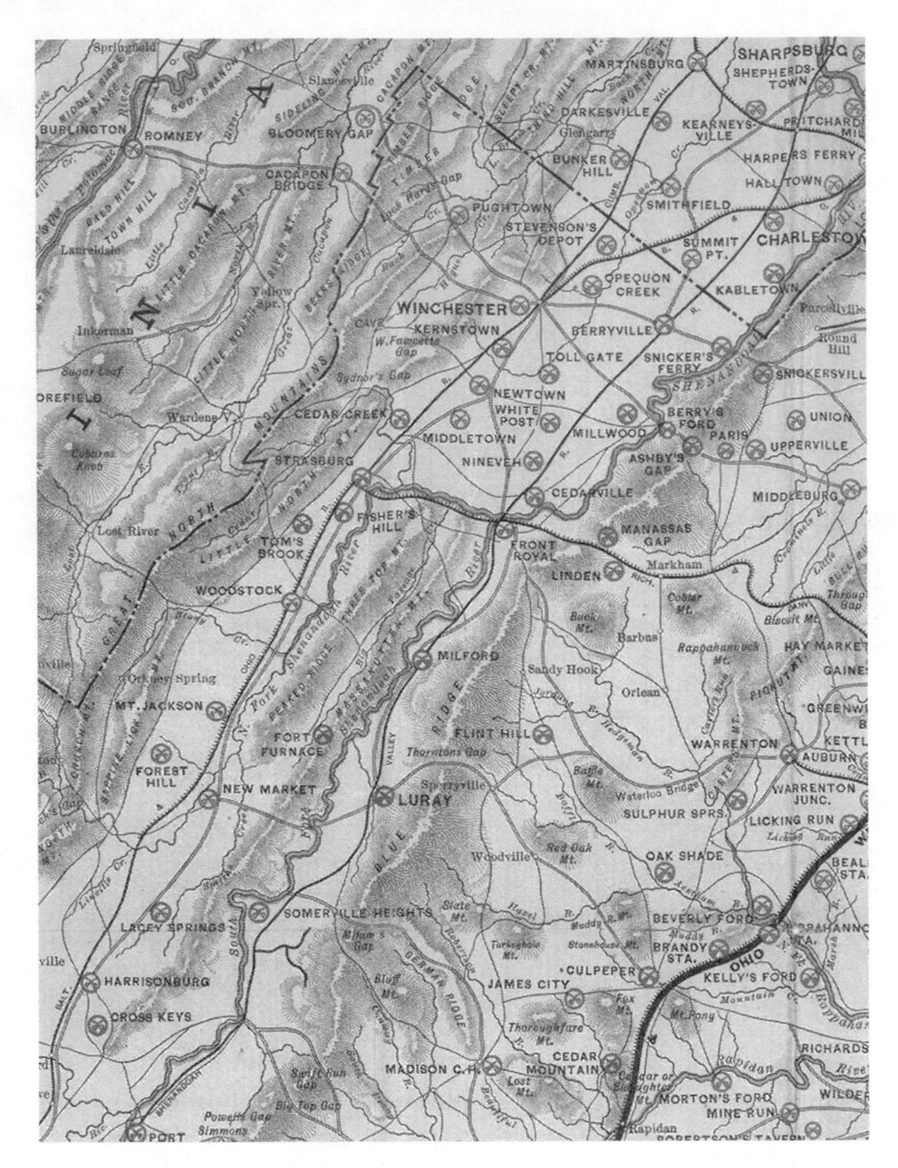

today. The good news is that most of these sites are public parkland, so you can visit them and learn from the experience.

• **Aldie, VA**, looks today much as it did 150 years ago. The centerpiece of the village is the Aldie Mill. This is the only functioning two-wheel grist mill in Virginia. It is owned and operated by the Northern Virginia Regional Park Authority, with demonstration grindings every weekend

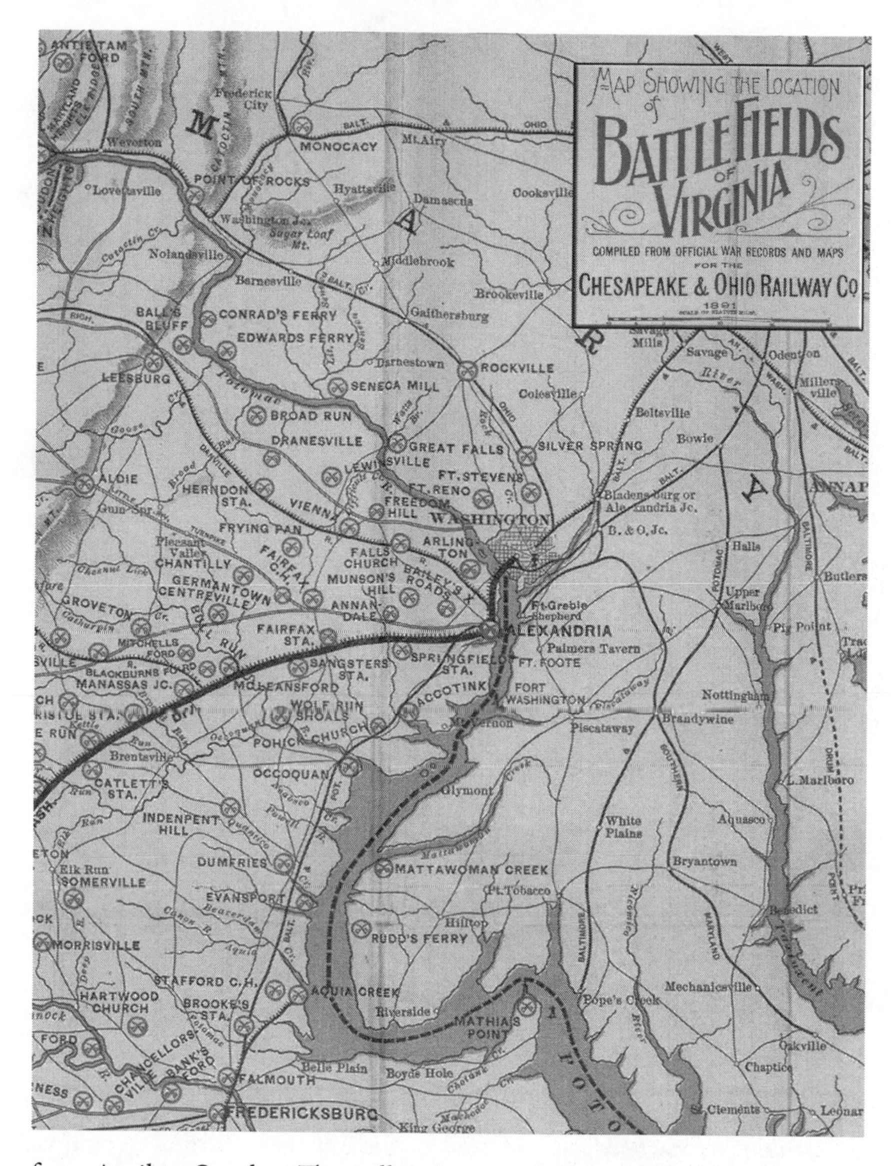

from April to October. The mill was restored in the 1980s and 1990s with the help of many generous donors when the property was owned by the Virginia Outdoors Foundation.

• **Antietam, MD**, is today preserved as the Antietam National Battlefield Park, owned and operated by the National Park Service outside Sharpsburg, Maryland.

• **Balls Bluff, VA**, just outside Leesburg, was the site of the Battle of Balls Bluff. Today this site is preserved as a battlefield park owned and operated by the Northern Virginia Regional Park Authority.

• **Brawner's Farm, VA**, is today a National Park Service site that is managed as part of the Manassas Battlefield Park.

• **Bristoe Station, VA**, is preserved today as Bristoe Station Battlefield Heritage Park, which is owned and operated by the Historic Preservation Division of Prince William County Virginia.

• **Bull Run (Manassas), VA**. See "Manassas."

• **Carlyle House, VA,** was used as a Union hospital throughout the Civil War taking in patients from many battles, including the Battle of Aldie. Today the Carlyle house is restored to its colonial period condition and is owned and operated as a museum by the Northern Virginia Regional Park Authority.

• **Cedar Creek, VA**, south of Winchester, is a battlefield area "partnership park" where the National Park Service works with The National Trust for Historic Preservation; Belle Grove, Inc.; Shenandoah Valley Battlefields Foundation; Cedar Creek Battlefield Foundation; and Shenandoah County, Virginia, to preserve and operate various areas of the battlefield.

• **Centerville Area Fortifications, VA**. During the Civil War the Bull Run stream that is the border between Fairfax County and Prince William County was a heavily fortified area. All along this area there were forts, camps, and artillery positions. Today most of this land is preserved in a natural state, owned and operated by the Northern Virginia Regional Park Authority. The 18-mile Bull Run–Occoquan trail runs from Bull Run Regional Park to Fountainhead Regional Park. It passes by and includes the site of Blackburn's Ford, an early battle, and many earthworks and archeological resources from this period.

• **Chancellorsville, VA**, outside Fredericksburg, is today preserved as part of the Fredericksburg and Spotsylvania National Military Park, owned and operated by the National Park Service.

• **Chantilly, VA**, the site of Mosby attack in the first chapter, is a few miles west of Chantilly on Rt. 50, and unmarked. However, this area of Rt. 50 is named "John Mosby Highway" and there are numerous historical markers along this scenic and historic road.

• **Chickahominy River Crossing, VA**, the site where General Stuart and his forces made a bridge to cross the Chickahominy River, is not a park. However, it is noted with a historic marker about one mile from the actual site. This is in New Kent County, to the east of Richmond.

• **Fort Craig, VA**, was one of a series of forts built around Washington, D.C. Fort Craig was located near the Pentagon. While this fort no longer exists, Arlington County maintains Fort C.F. Smith as a historic park in North Arlington as part of the same series of Civil War forts around Washington.

• **Gettysburg, PA**, the site of this most decisive battle in south-central Pennsylvania, is owned and operated by the National Park Service as the Gettysburg National Military Park.

• **Manassas (Bull Run), VA**, is preserved as the Manassas National Battlefield Park, owned and operated by the National Park Service. This site is just west of the Bull Run stream and northeast of the City of Manassas. This National Park encompasses the main battle area for both the First and Second Battle of Bull Run (Manassas). As was often the case during the Civil War, the North and South both had different names for the same battles.

• **Mt. Zion Church, VA**, is a historic church on Rt. 50 near the village of Aldie, at a crossroads called Gilbert's Corner. The church site built in 1851 was the first rendezvous point for Mosby's Rangers in January 1863. In July 1864 the church site and surrounding area were the site of a significant skirmish between Confederate cavalry under the command of Col. John Mosby and Union cavalry under the command of Major William Forbes. Today Mt. Zion Historic Church and the land across the road from the church are owned by the Northern Virginia Regional Park Authority.

• **Ox Hill, VA**, otherwise know as the Battle of Chantilly, is the most significant battle to take place in Fairfax County, Virginia. It took place as part of the continued fighting the day after the Second Battle of Bull Run (Manassas). Today a small, central part of this battlefield is preserved as Ox Hill Battlefield Park, which is owned and operated by the Fairfax County Park Authority.

• **Peninsula Campaign, VA**. Like the Shenandoah Valley Campaign, the Peninsula Campaign covers numerous battles over hundreds of miles. The Peninsula Campaign includes Yorktown and a large area of southeast Virginia up to and including the Richmond area. Today there are numerous historic markers and parks marking the locations of battles and fortifications constructed during this long campaign.

• **Seven-Day Battle, VA**, took place around Richmond. Today several sites associated with the Seven-Day Battle are protected as part of a series of properties owned by the National Park Service and operated as the Richmond National Battlefield Parks.

• **Shenandoah Valley Campaign, VA**, otherwise known as the "Valley Campaign," was fought in spring of 1862 from Winchester, Virginia, in the north to Staunton, Virginia, in the south. Today numerous historic markers and park sites dot the beautiful Shenandoah Valley to denote the events of the Civil War.

• **South Mountain, MD**, is found along the Blue Ridge Mountains in Maryland's Washington and Frederick counties. Today this is a back-country state park that includes sections of the Appalachian Trail. This is the area where the Battle of South Mountain occurred. There are no facilities in this area other than hiking tails.

• **Temple Hall Farm, VA**, is a farm established by a nephew of George Mason in 1810, north of Leesburg. In 1862 Lee's army passed in front of this farm on its way to Antietam. Today this is a farm park owned and operated by the Northern Virginia Regional Park Authority.

• **Upton Hill, VA**, is both the site of Confederate "Quaker guns" and observation tower in the early days of the war, and a main base camp for the Union, where the Iron Brigade spent some of its time. A visit to Fort Ramsay at Upton Hill by Julia Ward Howe resulted in the creation of the Battle Hymn of the Republic. Today Upton Hill is a popular park owned and operated by the Northern Virginia Regional Park Authority. Any physical evidence of the Civil War has been gone from the site for more than 100 years. Today this site features a water park, batting cages, and picnic areas. New historical interpretation of the Civil War significance of Upton Hill is planned for the 150th anniversary of the war.

• **Vicksburg, MS**, the main site of the Battlefield of Vicksburg, is owned by the National Park Service and operated as the Vicksburg National Military Park in west-central Mississippi.

• **The Willard Hotel, Washington, DC**, is the place where General Charles Stone was the night he was arrested in 1861. Today the Willard Hotel still stands along Pennsylvania Avenue in the nation's capital. The Willard is owned and operated by Intercontinental Hotels and Resorts.

APPENDIX C

Historical and Other Sources

Readers interested in acquiring further information about the stories presented in this book are invited to consult the following references, which served as the source material for *Lead Like a General.*

Introduction

Tzu, Sun. *The Art of War.* Translated by Gary Gagliardi (2007). Seattle, WA: Clearbridge Publishing.

Chapter 1

Mosby, J. (1887). *War Reminiscences and Stuarts Cavalry Campaign.* New York: Dodd Mead and Company.

Pentland, A. (2010, January-February). Defend your research: We can measure the power of charisma. *Harvard Business Review.*

Rath, T. & Conchie, B. (2008). *Strengths-Based Leadership.* New York: Gallup Press.

Chapter 2

Andrade, E.B. & Ariely, D. (2009, May). Organizational behavior and human decision processes. *Elsevier Journal 109(1).*

Cozzens, P. (ed.). (2010, April). The war was a grievous error: General James Longstreet speaks his mind." *Civil War Times*, pp. 32–39.

Chapter 3

Herrmann, N. (1996). Herrmann whole brain model. The Whole Brain Business Book. New York: McGraw-Hill.

McPherson, J. (1988). Battle Cry of Freedom. New York: Oxford University Press.

Chapter 4

Rath, T. (2008). *Strength-Based Leadership.* (Gallup Press, New York).

Sears, S. (1998). *Chancellorsville.* New York: Houghton Mifflin.

Tarbell, I.M. (1900). The Life of Abraham Lincoln (Vol. 3). New York: Lincoln Historical Society.

Chapter 5

Hogart, W. (1906). A medal of honor. *War Talks in Kansas.* Kansas City, MO: Franklin Hudson Publishing.

Chapter 6

Amabile, T., & Kramer, S. (2010, January-February). The HBR list: Breakthrough ideas of 2010." *Harvard Business Review.*

Cooke, J.E. (1866). *Stonewall Jackson: A Military Biography.* New York: D. Appleton & Co.

Chapter 7

Gottlieb, H. Creating the Future. http://hildygottlieb.com/

Holien, K. (1996). *Battle at Ball's Bluff.* Orange, VA: Moss Publications.

Morgan, J. (2004). *A Little Short of Boats:The Fight at Ball's Bluff and Edward's Ferry.* Fort Mitchell, KY: Ironclad Publishing.

Pozen, R. (2010, December). The case for professional boards. *Harvard Business Review.*

Stone, C. (1887). Washington on the eve of the war. In: *Battles and Leaders of the Civil War, Vol. I.* New York: The Century Company.

Stone, C. (1862, Nov. 5). Letter from Stone to Lossing. Schoff Collection (Stone MS). University of Michigan. Cullum 2, nos. 1139 and 1237.

Chapter 8

Cooke, J.E. (1867). *Wearing of the Gray.* New York: E.B. Trent & Co.

Cooke, J.E. (1866). *Stonewall Jackson: A Military Biography.* New York: D. Appleton & Co.

Ishida, J. (2008). Decisiveness (OSIPP Discussion Paper 08E002). Osaka University School of International Public Policy. Available from http://econpapers.repec.org/paper/ospwpaper/08e002.htm

Chapter 9

Grant. U.S. (2005). *The Papers of Ulysses S. Grant (Vol. 28)* edited by John Simon. Carbondale, IL: Southern Illinois University Press.

Hanaburgh, D.H. (1894). *History of the One Hundred and Twenty-Eighth Regiment: New York.* New York: Enterprise Publishing.

Pentland, A. (2010, January-February). Defend your research: We can measure the power of charisma. *Harvard Business Review.*

Sheridan, P. (2007). *The Memoirs of General P.H. Sheridan* (originally published in 1888). New York: Cosimo Inc.

Sheridan, P. (1991). *Civil War Memoirs* (first published in 1888). New York: Bantam Books.

Chapter 10

-----. (1911). *Indiana at Antietam, Report of the Indiana Antietam Monument Commission.* Indianapolis, IN: The Aetna Press.

Dawes, R. (1890). On the right at Antietam." In: Hunter, R. (ed.). *Sketches of War History 1861-1865.* Cincinnati, OH: The Commandery.

Gittell, J.H., Seidner, R., & Wimbush, J. (2010, March-April). A relational model of how high-performance work systems work. *Organizational Science 21(2),* pp. 490–506.

Hogart, W. (1906). A medal of honor. *War Talks in Kansas.* Kansas City, MO: Franklin Hudson Publishing.

Nolan, A. & Vipond, S. (1998). *Giants in Their Tall Black Hats: Essays on the Iron Brigade.* Bloomington, IN: Indiana University Press.

Walker, F. (1897). General Gibbon in the second corps. In: Blakeman, N. (ed.). *Personal Recollections of the War of the Rebellion.* New York: G.P. Putnam's Sons.

Chapter 11

Kim, C. & Mauborgne, R. (2005). *Blue Ocean Strategy.* Boston MA: Harvard Business School Press.

Munson, J. (1906). *Reminiscences of a Mosby Guerrilla.* New York: Moffat, Yard & Co.

Williamson, J. (1896). *Mosby's Rangers: A Record of the Operations of the Forty-Third Battalion Virginia Cavalry.* New York: Ralph Kenyon Publishing.

Chapter 12

Buckingham, M. (2001). Strengthfinder. *Now, Discover Your Strengths.* New York: The Free Press.

Herrmann, N. (1996). Herrmann whole brain model. *The Whole Brain Business Book.* New York: McGraw-Hill.

APPENDIX D

Battlefield Maps

What follows is a larger look at the respective battlefield maps presented in this book.

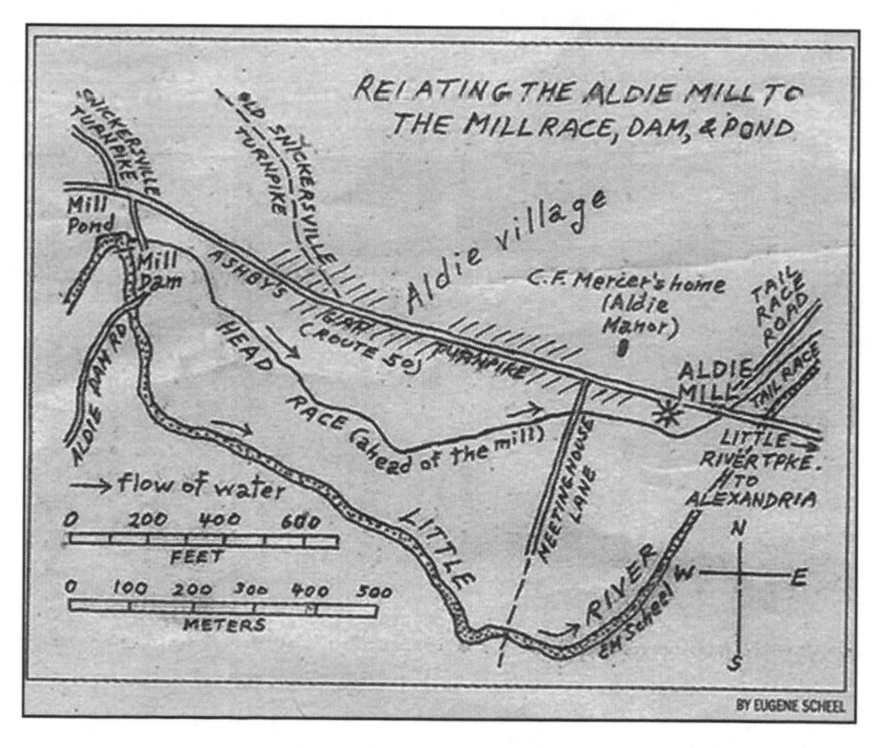

ALDIE, VA

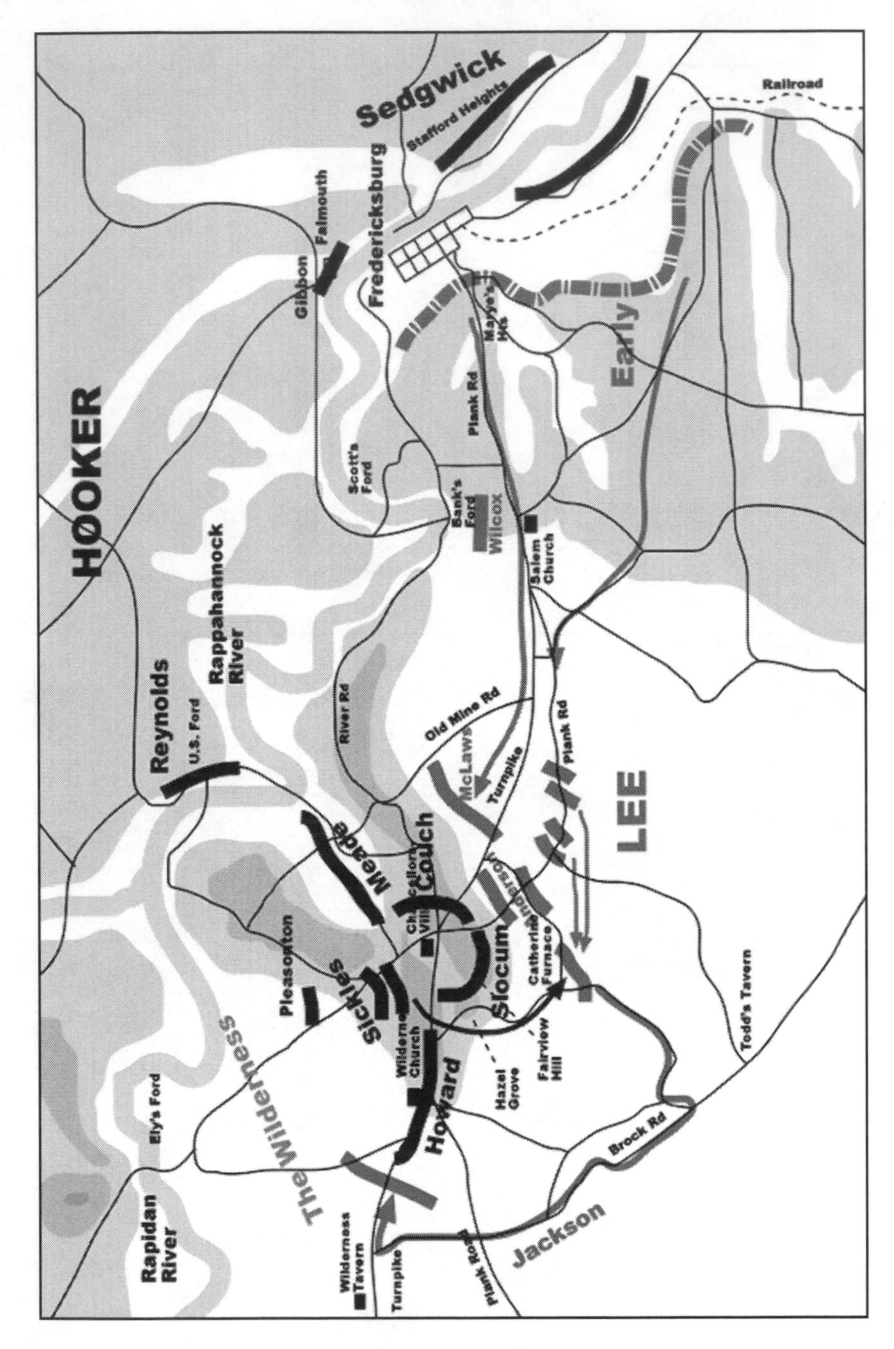

Battle of Chancellorsville

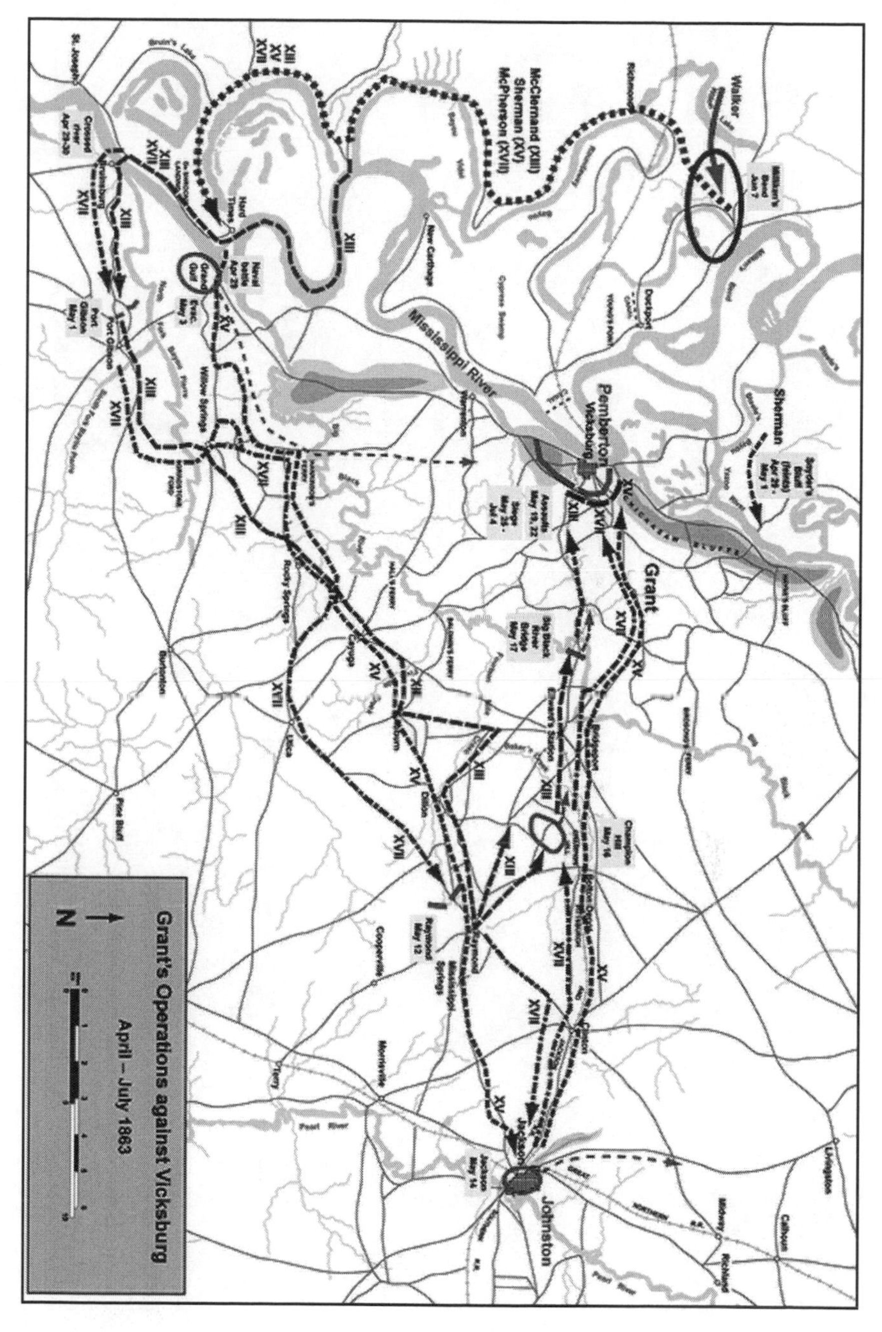

BATTLE OF
VICKSBURG

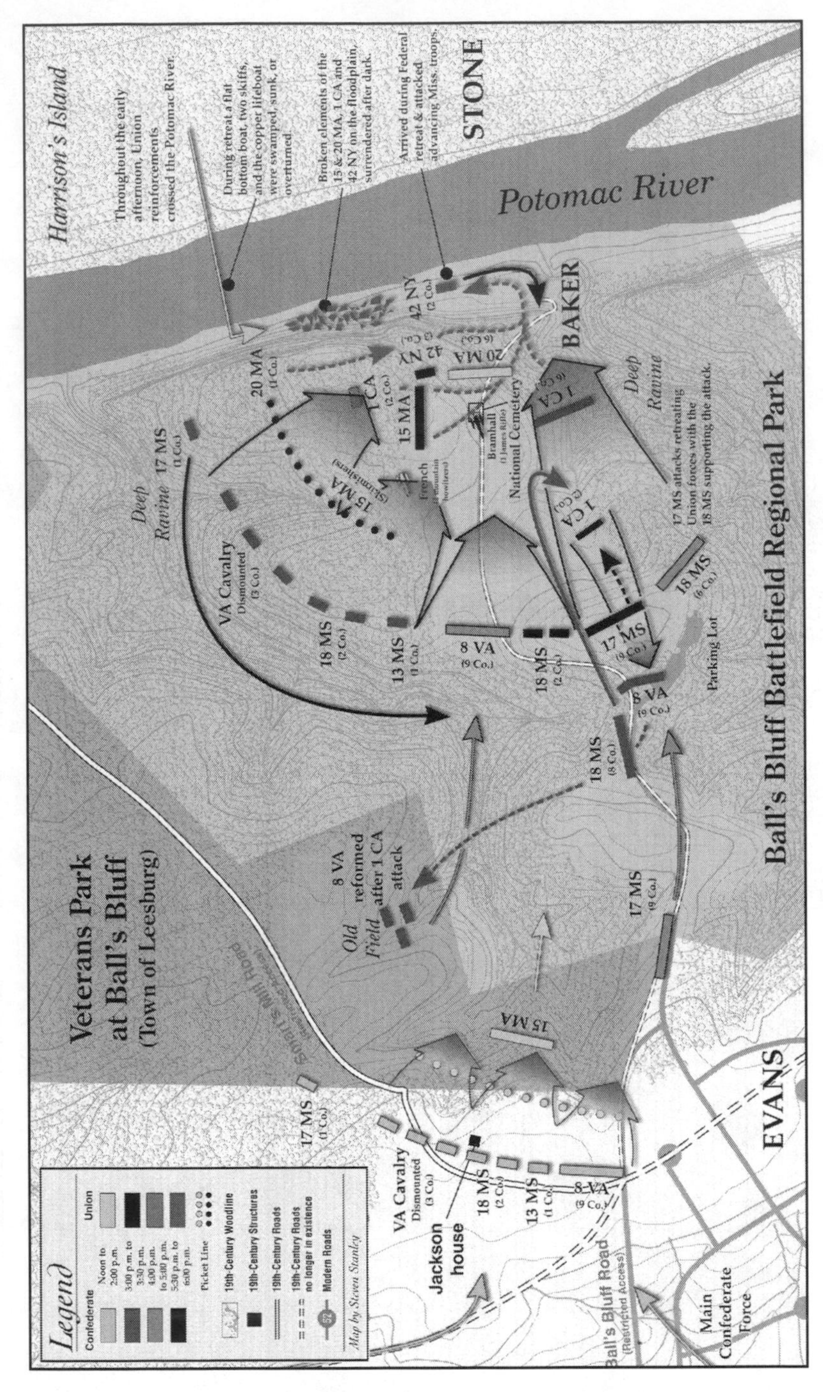

BATTLE OF BALL'S BLUFF

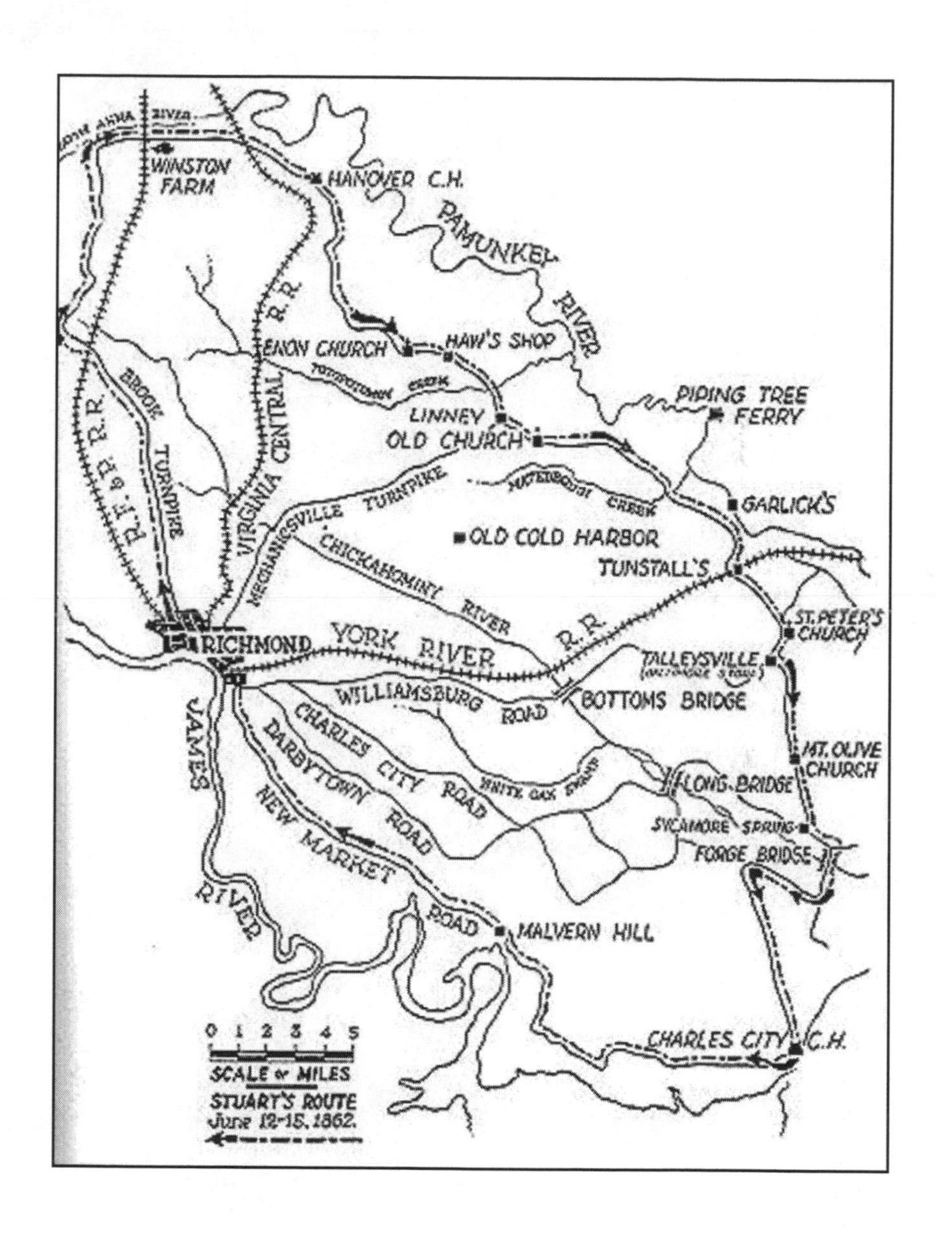

Stuart's Ride Around McLellan

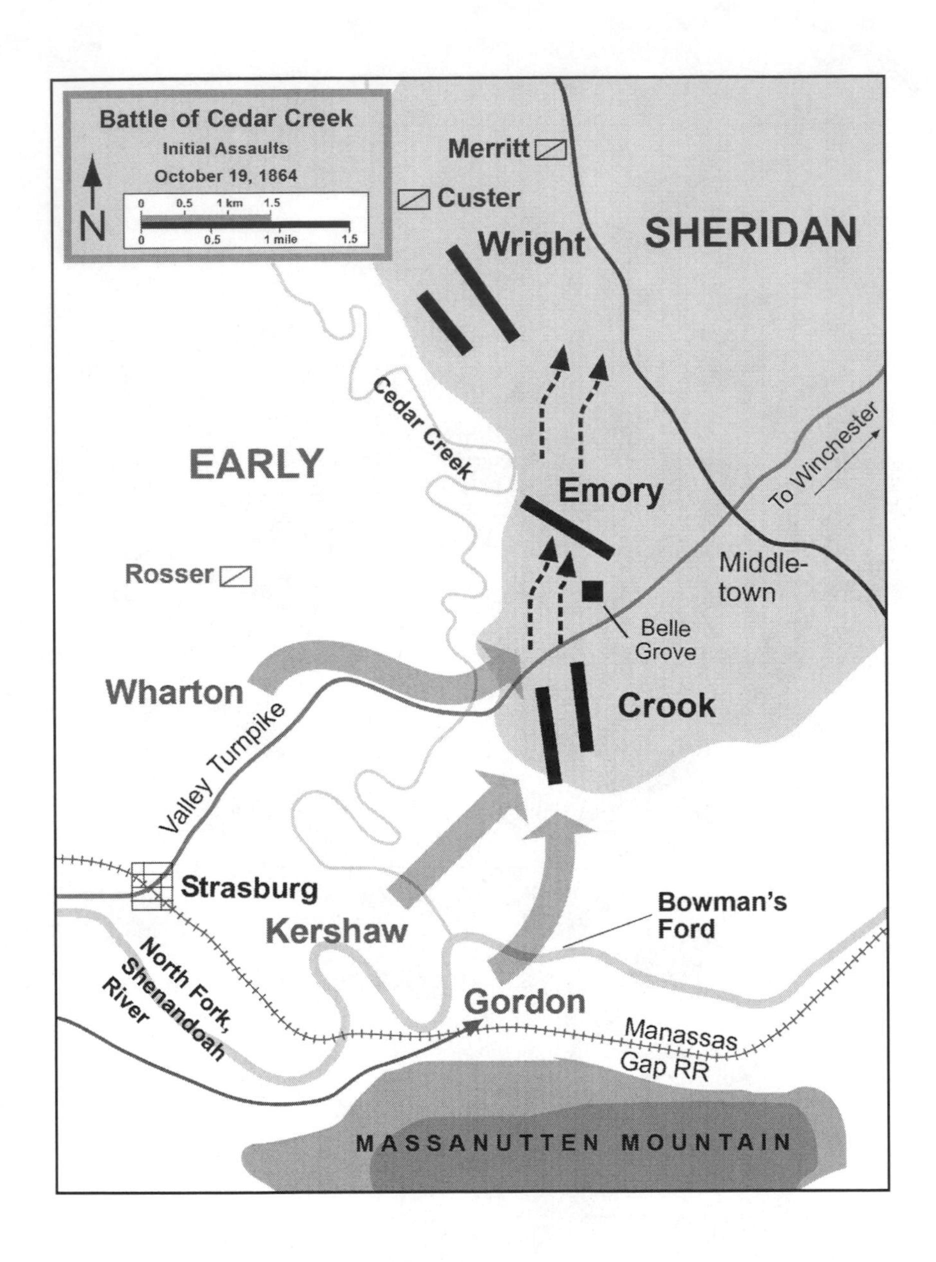

Battle of
Cedar Creek

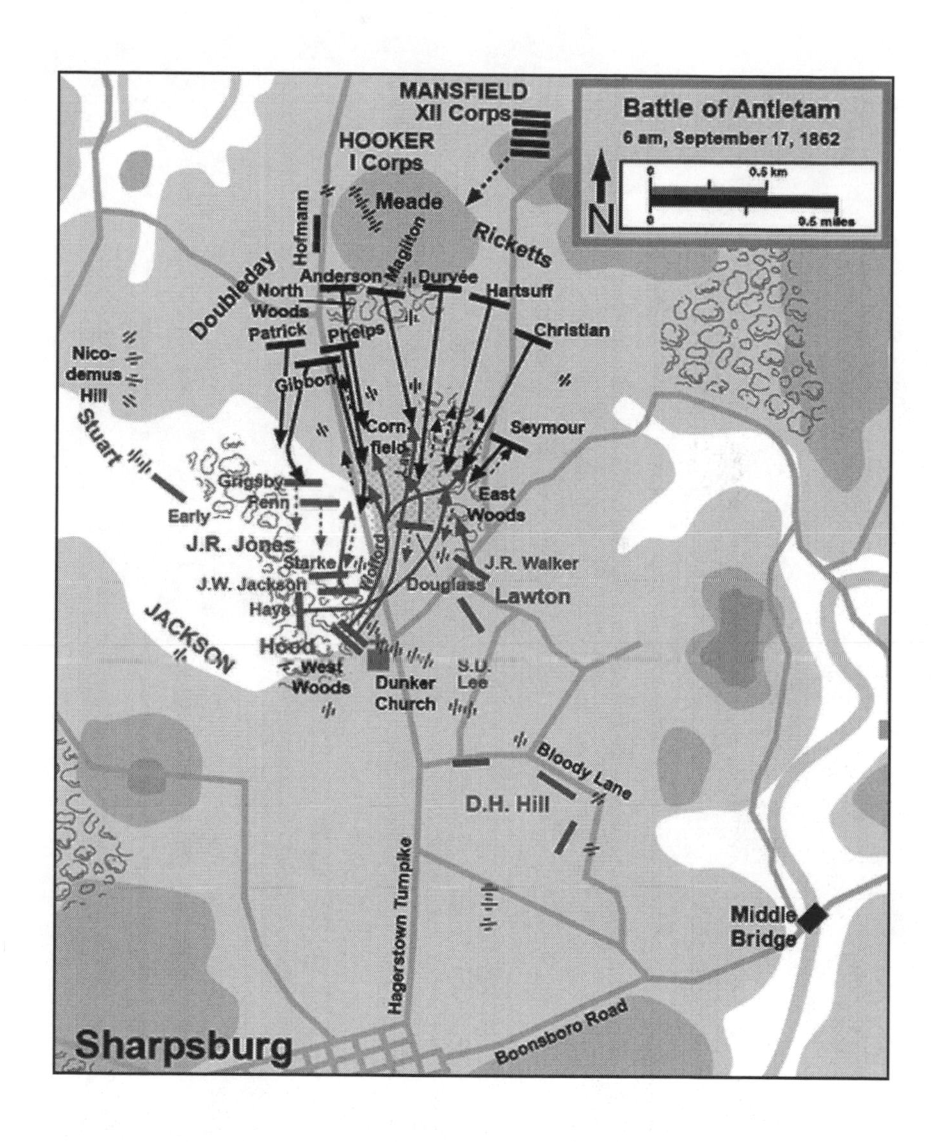

BATTLE OF
ANTIETAM

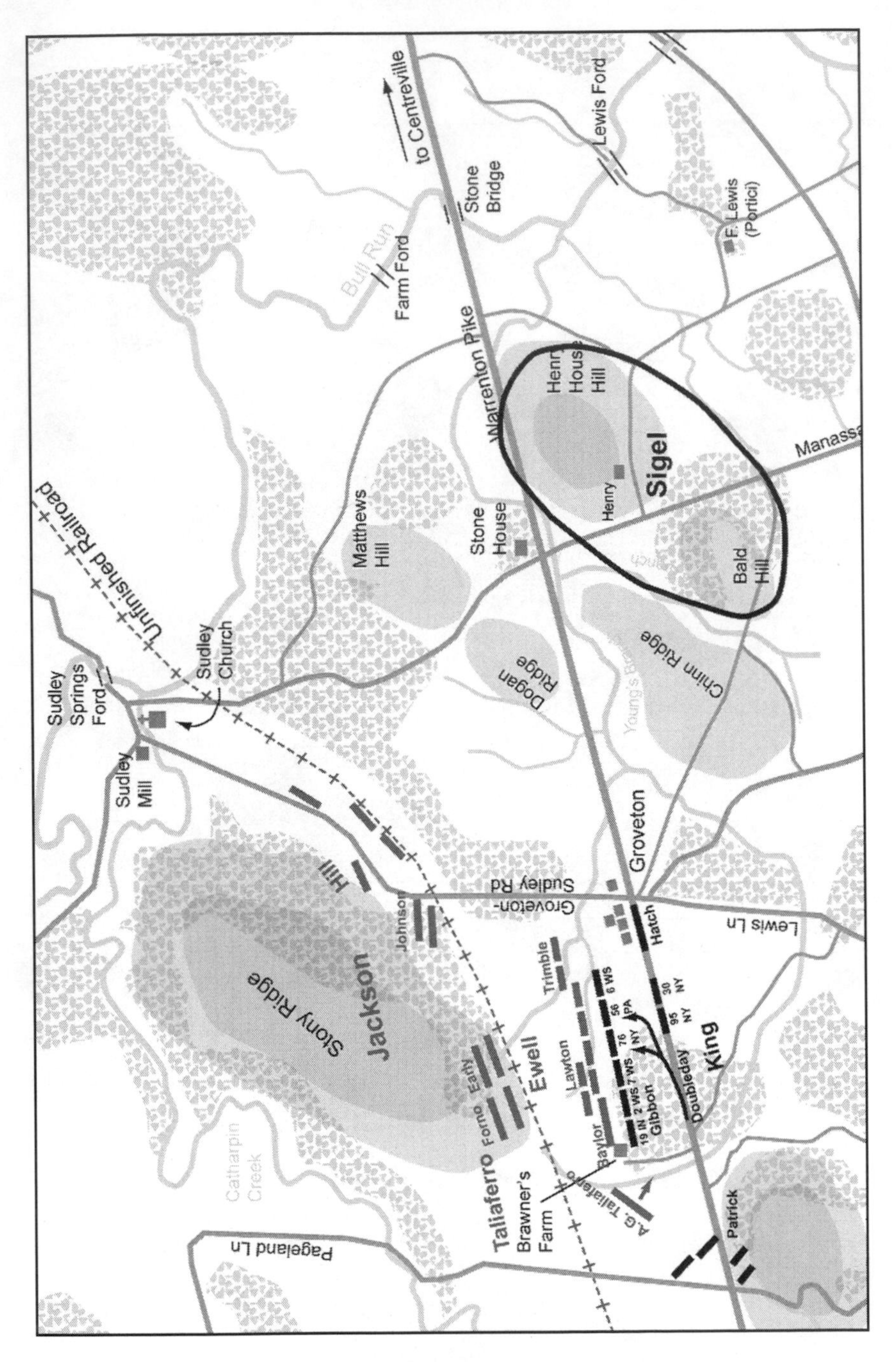

BATTLE OF
BRAWNER'S FARM

About the Author

Paul Gilbert has been in leadership roles in governmental, nonprofit and private sector organizations. He has served on the governance boards of six organizations.

Gilbert holds a bachelor's degree in politics from St. Andrews College and a master's degree in interdisciplinary studies, with a focus on conflict resolution and public policy, from George Mason University. Gilbert has studied organizational change, leadership, communication, and innovation through the Aresty Institute of Executive Education at the Wharton School of Business.

As Executive Director of the Northern Virginia Regional Park Authority Gilbert oversees the management of a diverse system of public lands and facilities which include numerous historic sites.

Gilbert is adjunct faculty at George Mason University, and on the Board of Regents for the School of Revenue Development and Management at Oglebay.

Gilbert has written articles on leadership, history and environmental issues for magazines and newspapers. He also writes a blog on issues related to the Northern Virginia Regional Park Authority.

Made in the USA
Charleston, SC
25 May 2011